F

9/50

Film Soleil

D.K. Holm

www.pocketessentials.com

This edition published in Great Britain 2005 by Pocket Essentials
P.O. Box 394, Harpenden, Herts, AL5 1XJ, UK

Distributed in the USA by Trafalgar Square Publishing
P.O. Box 257, Howe Hill Road, North Pomfret, Vermont 05053

A CIP catalogue record for this book is available from the British Library.

ISBN 1–904048–50–1

2 4 6 8 10 9 7 5 3 1

Book typeset by Avocet Typeset, Chilton, Aylesbury, Bucks
Printed and bound by Cox & Wyman, reading, Berkshire

Acknowledgements

There is nothing like undertaking a project of such scope and detail as this one to reveal one's own ignorance. To that end this author must salute the following helpers: Mark Christensen, Desiree French, Helaine Garren, Britta Gordon, Charles and Ingrid Gordon, Damon Houx, Anne Hughes, Shawn Levy, Patti Lewis, Cynthia Lopez, Andrea Marsden, Gregg Morris, Michael Russell, Charles Schwenk (a great scholar and a great human being), Steffen Silvis, Sam Smith, Robert Wederquist (DVDJournal.com), as well as the Multnomah County Library, Portland State University Library, Powell's Books, the Internet Movie Data Base, and the numerous transitory DVD publicists who provided discs. Acknowledgment is also due Ion Mills for the courage to be innovative. Special notice must be paid to Chris Ryall, my editor at Kevin Smith's adjunct website, MoviePoopShoot.com, where small portions of a few of these reviews appeared. Since the start of this century, Chris has been a supportive editor and a great friend, and so to him this book is gratefully dedicated.

Contents

1. Introduction: Film Noir Vs. Film Soleil

Do genres really change? Can they evolve, mutate, and even improve? And if so, when and how? Do we, as consumers really *want* genres to change? Or are we more delighted by variations within a stable template? And at what point, after a genre has changed, do we give in and admit that what we are dealing with is a wholly *new* genre, with its own formulae, conventions, prejudices, and viewer expectations?

Take the musical. Speaking in broad strokes, its evolution is based partly on technological changes, and partly on shifts in pop culture tastes. Stage musicals had been adapted even to the silent screen, but with the advent of sound, initially movie musicals were mostly set within the musical theater world. Reflecting a movement toward realism found in the theater, movie musicals makers in the 1950s began to set their films in non-musical settings and tell serious stories, as seen as early as *Showboat* and later in *West Side Story*. With the rise of youth culture in the mid-1950s, musicals began a shift toward pop tunes and live concert performances. By the end of the century weird hybrids such as *Moulin Rouge* were perfectly acceptable and understandable to both fans of movies and of musicals.

Hollywood movie comedy also has a complex history. Again, in reductive terms, its evolution can be traced from highly visual slapstick in the silent era to verbal "screwball"

9

wit with the advent of sound, then to the dominance of youth culture during the mid-century war years, as manifested in the partnerships of Abbott and Costello, the Three Stooges, Martin and Lewis, then shifting to the rise of sketch-comedy-based movies targeted to specific demographics, usually based on stories from the magazine *National Lampoon* or characters and stars from *Saturday Night Live*.

The fate of the western is the worst of all. Once arguably *the* American movie genre, the one in which Hollywood could talk to Americans about their shared history, the western could manifest itself simultaneously in both low-grade actioners and prestige productions without harming the essence of the genre itself. In fact, the western became so popular in the 1950s that prime time television was inundated with programs (*Cheyenne, Sugarfoot*), most of them from Warner Bros. studios. So many, in fact, that it was as if the American public became so surfeited on the genre that in the 1970s, 1980s, and 1990s viewers couldn't bear to expose themselves to it anymore. Worse, younger audiences appeared to have little interest in the western, to the point that what once was traditionally thought of, throughout the 20th Century, as America's premiere genre could barely be said to exist at the start of the 21st Century.

That is certainly the problem facing fans of film noir from the 1970s on. Had noir evolved into a new genre? Since "true" film noir, that is black and white crime films, ended, officially or not, in 1958, can so-called film noirs made after that time frame be anything but pastiches, homage, or parodies?

And is noir even a genre to begin with? On the one hand you can have a film such as *The Postman Always Rings Twice* (Tay Garnett, 1946) with virtually none of the visual cues associated with noir (Venetian blinds, harsh shadows, dark streets at night) and all of its narrative cues (a femme fatale, love triangles, crimes of passion and profit), while *Reign of Terror* (AKA, *The Black Book*, Anthony Mann, 1949) has none of the narrative cues yet all of the genre's visual hallmarks. "Defining" noir is a task more like classifying architecture. A bungalow is still a house but it is not like a thatched roof Tudor house; we see the differences that link the two houses to their individual categories, yet grasp their broad similarities to the larger base set to which they all belong. We're able to juggle and categorize all this in our mind and the more examples we have at hand the more refined individual definitions become.

Critics ranging from Raymond Durgnat to James Naremore have wrestled with just what exactly it is when we speak about film noir. Naremore asserted that noir "functions rather like big words such as *romantic* or *classic*. An Ideological concept with a history all its own, it can be used to describe a period, a movement, and a recurrent style" (in *More Than Night*). Paul Schrader, back when he was still a movie reviewer rather than a director, defined noir as "a period." Durgnat gave, in passing, perhaps the best definition of noir in his book *Jean Renoir*: noir, he wrote, is "a crime thriller with a pessimistic, cynical, sardonic approach and mood." You can get a good sense of the basic noir ingredients from the titles of the plethora of noir books printed since the 1980s. Lonely streets, dead ends, detours, darkness, dark cities, anxiety, crime, the past – few of these iconic components contribute to film soleil. In soleil, noir returns to its roots in westerns, and all genres meld into one.

That leaves the genre open to a lot of morphing. The author of this book is himself uncertain of just what, exactly, noir happens to be, and hesitates to enter very well trodden intellectual ground, sifted over by scores of previous critics in the 100-plus books already written about noir. When I embarked on this project I determined that noir was not a genre but rather more a set of signifiers linked by general and overriding narrative genre conventions. Right now, however, I think that it actually might be a genre, if for no other reason than that it can be replicated in different variations with audiences still recognising a given film as a noir. After publication, I may well revert back to the "mood" thesis.

Many aspects considered proprietary to noir are often "in the air." For example, the noir policiers of the 1940s, with their documentary style elucidations of procedures – as in *Call Northside 777* – and the films produced by Mark Hellinger and Louis De Rochemont, are really very like military films of the 1940s, such as *Destination Tokyo* (Delmer Daves, 1943) which begins with details of bureaucratic procedures.

In any event, it is the argument of this book that noir *did* change, sprouting a sub-genre that grew to independence and became the premier crime genre of its time. This new genre emerged in the mid-1970s, but had roots going back to noirs of the 1940s and earlier. For want of a better term I call it "film soleil" to distinguish it from noir proper. Although derived from noir, films in this genre have obviously different settings and in some cases different concerns.

Other books and essays settle for the label neo-noir, with which to gather up post 1960s crime dramas derived from noir (though somewhere in one of his reviews from the 1980s J. Hoberman of the *Village Voice* calls the genre *film blanc*). But because film soleil is significantly different in its attitude to crime, its portrayal of sex, and its visual strategies, I prefer to think of it as a genre unto itself.

2. Evil Under the Sun: Film Soleil Defined

How easy it is to evoke the tones of traditional film noir. Street lamps. Dark alleys. Trench coats. Shadows slanting from Venetian blinds in dusty offices where the scent of death hangs in a plume of coiling cigarette smoke. A mysterious woman with golden hair and stiletto heels pleads her case to an impassive PI who is fighting inner turmoil, a man soon to be desperately on the run to nowhere.

Noir has been condensed to an easily cataloged visual vocabulary that disguises its subtlety; and in fact, the multiple and sometimes-incompatible variations of noir can, as noted previously, render the genre difficult to define. As Wittgenstein might suggest in a lighter moment, no noir has all the genre's visual and narrative tropes, but every noir must have some of them.

Yet as the culture ages and reconfigures itself, so too do its popular genres, and the same Wittgensteinian principal holds true for film soleil, a relatively recent variation or offshoot of noir. Reverse all those frozen noir images. Change the darkened street to a dry, sun-beaten road. Convert the dark alley to a highway mercilessly cutting through a parched, sagebrush-filled desert. Give the woman cowboy boots and stick her in a speeding car, driven by a deranged man whose own biological drives lead him less often to sex than to fights over money. Institute these changes and you have film soleil. The string of sunlit crime films officially began in 1984 with the release of *Blood Simple*, joined shortly by *Kill Me Again* (1989), *After Dark, My Sweet* (1990), and *One False Move* (1992) – all heralding the arrival of a new cinematic style.

The critical breast beats with excitement when out of the cultural ether and the 400-plus films Hollywood releases annually there comes a brand spanking new genre. In the 1980s, one did begin to take shape. On its surface, film soleil is a simple reversal of film noir – night becomes day, city becomes country, lush love becomes raw and hate-filled sex. Tighter "indie" style shooting budgets that require "closet drama" size casts and simple sets, a flood of neophyte directors on the market, and fluctuations in shooting practices all combined with a reaction to the Reagan 1980s, to give rise to film soleil. It's possible that eventually, film soleil, a sub-genre of a sub-genre, will go the way of rural comedies and airmail delivery films. But for now it's here, and over the course of some 25 years appears to have longevity.

Arguably the most passionately followed of all film genres, the urban psychological crime drama, dubbed by French cineaste Nino Frank as film noir, has been commercially moribund for many years, while its films, made roughly between 1940 and 1959, live on in the VCRs and DVD players of passionate addicts and in a steady stream of books and articles that find the genre suitable terrain for diverse critical approaches. Other genres and mainstream films have easily utilised noir's appeal to male self-pity, its fantasies of lonely moral purity versus creatively cruel evil, its additions to cultural signatures of cool, and its skewed view of sexuality, one that is both frank and cunningly muted. But few of these modern borrowers have blended the elements of dark cinema into such a heady, flavorful cocktail.

Traces of film noir still cling to the film soleil like last night's cigarettes on the fingertips and shirt. Male self-pity, money, guns, and women remain the basic ingredients. Film soleil takes the many fundamental elements of noir and, so to speak, turns on the lights. That which is threatening in the shadows comes to seem more unremittingly bare and relentless under the sword-like rays of the sun.

If traditional film noir is night and shadows, then film soleil is daytime and sunny. If noir is luscious black and white photography, then soleil is a bow to the inevitability of colour. If noir is New York, soleil is Los Angeles. If noir is Chandler and Hammett, soleil is Jim Thompson and Charles Willeford. Money is a moral compass in noir, an indice of a character's depravity, while in soleil greed is good, greed works. If noir is oneiric, drugged, sapped, then soleil is clear, wakeful, sober, and cunning. If noir is booze and cigarettes, soleil is LSD and cocaine. If noir is the city, soleil is the country, but "bad" country, of raised pitchforks, heat, suspicion, and the dusty land where dreams end. If noir is the art of the double cross, soleil is the triple and quadruple cross. If noir has its roots in B horror films and double bill fillers, then soleil has its roots in direct-to-video and erotic thrillers.

Noir now has an ambiguous position within contemporary film. When attempts at traditional noirs are made, they are set in the past, such as the Robert Mitchum–Dick Richards *Farewell, My Lovely* from 1975, or evoke cinematic predecessors but without the constrictions of the Production Code, as in Lawrence Kasdan's *Body Heat* (1981), which is more of a soleil. But advances in colour photography can only be one cause of traditional noir's demise. After all, noir's visual components, human and otherwise, ultimately only serve to make the genre's moral and narrative points.

As noir fell, film soleil rose, though not yet in an easily named cubbyhole. The key transitional film from noir to its new, sunnier incarnations is Roman Polanski and Robert Towne's *Chinatown* in 1974. Both an *hommage* and a playful variation on noir, *Chinatown* alternated images of urban squalor (shade) with those of the new frontier (sun).

Just as Herman Melville challenged western conventions in *Moby Dick*, by choosing the colour white to symbolise evil, young filmmakers began overturning our expectations about where to find evil in their soleils. Rising filmmakers may have gravitated toward film soleil because, not only is it a genre that packs the kind of shock that comes when you overturn a box in your backyard and find a dead rat underneath (the Lynchian perspective), but sunlight is cheaper.

Film soleil is more than just a variation on noir. It represents the weaving together of many strands, foremost among them the work of Jim Thompson. That Thompson's books have proved a rich mine for soleil directors should come as no surprise to those familiar with earlier adaptations, such as Sam Peckinpah and Walter Hill's original *The Getaway* (1972). The prolific writer who was eventually reduced to *Ironside* novelisations and a "mercy casting" in *Farewell, My Lovely* is perhaps the most influential figure in film soleil, providing the setting, the women, and the heroes for actual soleils, and inspiring a host of mimics. As often happens the French were there first. Bertrand Tavernier's *Coup De Torchon* (1981), adapted from Thompson's novel *POP. 1280*, and transplanted from the American south to Northern Africa, nevertheless captures in its *Yojimbo*-style story the essential Thompsonian hero, a man surrounded by conniving people who all conclude that he is too stupid to catch on to their blatant machinations.

This Thompsonesque figure is usually situated in a story that draws for inspiration upon an assortment of earlier heist films, such as Phil Karlson's Reno-set *5 Against the House* (1955) and Stanley Kubrick's *The Killing* (1956), whose script Thompson wrote, as well as the "road thriller," from *Detour* (1945) and *Gun Crazy* (1949) to its more philosophical manifestations, such as *Badlands* (1973). The genre also alludes to – or emerges from the same primordial soup as – two other important strains of popular film. Desert sci-fi from the 1950s such as *Them!* (Gordon Douglas, 1954), *Tarantula* (Jack Arnold, 1955), and *The Brain Eaters* (Bruno Ve Sota, 1958) established the eeriness of that vast, lonely landscape. *Invasion of the Body Snatchers* (Don Siegel, 1956) blended bright California sun with dark closets and caves, reversing what is now the current trajectory by importing noir in the desert instead of the desert into noir. The dark "psychological" westerns of Anthony Mann and Budd Boetticher, with a little Raoul Walsh thrown in (*Pursued*, 1947), provide models for getting the most, narratively and thematically, from small casts and limited settings.

The slow and inexorable march of film soleil to its current pre-eminence finds benchmarks, either thematic or visual, in *The Wages of Fear* (1952), *Touch of Evil* (1958), and *Purple Noon* (1960). Robert Ryan takes on the mantle of a pre-soleil icon with his appearance in numerous precursors, including *Inferno* (1953). This little seen Roy Ward Baker 3D film, which also anticipates desert sci-fi, casts Ryan as a wealthy husband dumped in the desert as part of a murder plot by wife Rhonda Fleming. He also pops up in *Bad Day at Black Rock* (1955), which draws upon that strand of noir concerned with troubled veterans, planting them in the desert waste.

Unlike noir homages of the 1970s, soleil takes a selection of traditional elements and shapes them to reflect modern concerns. These elements can be easily cataloged.

Guns. *Noir* didn't fetishise or phallicise firearms. That's a modern obsession. The fistfight, which is the usual action climax of so many simple crime films, doesn't appear much in film soleil. In most modern action movies, the gun is the *un*equaliser, a symbol of a basic unfairness, of the power that combatants seek to have over each other. Now, it's the firefight that is the culmination of narrative tension in most popular films. In soleil, however, it's only an occasional capper, such as in *One False Move*. Most film soleil take a surprisingly modest approach to gunplay. Confrontations are psychological and emotional, as at the triumph of evil at the end of the *Grifters* or a stud's sexual enslavement at the climax of the *Hot Spot*.

Money. It's still the American grail, but more important than ever in the aftermath of 1980s greed and desperation and the current economic crash. Money continues to fuel the plots of most soleils – *The Grifters, One False Move, After Dark, My Sweet, Kill Me Again, Confidence* – as it did in many noirs.

Villains. You also find a tougher breed of renegades, rogues, and gangster wannabes in film soleil. The disparity between rich and poor has regained Dickensian proportions, and the world is a meaner place; the home-invading, cop-killing drug-peddler trio in *One False Move* is an especially frightening example. Gangsters are more ruthless – for example, Pat Hingle in *The Grifters* and James Woods in *The Getaway* and *Against All Odds* – and roam freely in a world of their own making, a fishbowl of wealth and privilege that others are striving to enter.

Women. The women of film soleil are also driven by the new selfishness. Like lottery players, they pin all their hopes on one big killing – which can end up requiring a series of actual killings. Knowing that as a commodity sex is now more valuable than ever, the slick soleil dames – Jennifer Rubin in *Delusion*, Joanna Whalley-Kilmer in *Kill Me Again*, Linda Fiorentino in *The Last Seduction* – are the ruthless mercs so often associated with noir, but who are here usually permitted to triumph in soleil. There are a few nice women, the equivalents of Robert Mitchum's vanilla girlfriend in *Out of the Past*, such as Mimi Rodgers in *White Sands*, but they tend to be minimised; surely the female to which the genre ultimately aspires is Drew Barrymore's troubled, amoral but fair vixen in Tamra Davis' *Guncrazy*.

Heroes. If soleil's leather-clad or skimpily-dressed women are becoming gutsier and franker, the men are shrinking. They are weaker, dumber, poorer; their sorry state is only occasionally mitigated by a wit and self-reflection that remains hidden, in true Thompsonian fashion, to all but the viewer. Reckless and compromised, John Getz in *Blood Simple*, John Cusack in *The Grifters*, Bill Paxton in *One False Move*, and Gary Oldman in *Romeo is Bleeding*, inspire in the viewer little faith that they can extricate themselves from a tight situation – and they usually don't.

Bad marriages. Perhaps the true subject of film soleil, the bad marriage takes center stage when, as in for example *Kalifornia*, the feel good, self-help culture meets the serial killer on a friendless highway to nowhere. But film soleil has also added to the panoply of noir-derived crime drama elements with variations drawn from other genres.

Cars. The wide-open spaces find utterly disparate people battling each other in cramped autos. Whereas noir used the car, if at all, as a transitional space for conversation, in soleil it is the psychodramatic prelude to the killing ground. In Carl Colpaert's *Delusion* (1990), perhaps the quintessential soleil, Jim Metzler, Jennifer Rubin, and Kyle Secor play mind games that no one of them fully grasps, and in *Kalifornia*, two separate, troubled relationships intersect like a car wreck.

The road. As in the road film, the highway invites movement, but as an antidote to facing oneself, and toward a goal that too often turns out to be illusory.

Trailer parks. This pervasive and fascinating American symbol joins the promise of movement with almost inescapable stasis, as shown in *Guncrazy* and *Kalifornia*. It has spawned a genre unto itself, represented by *Hold Me Thrill Me Kiss Me* (Joel Hershman, 1992) and *Gas, Food, Lodging* (Allison Anders, 1992).

The desert. This vast American landscape, in which one is everywhere and nowhere at the same time, which offers promise and death simultaneously, is crucial to the concerns of film soleil, where evil is open and out front to those who allow themselves to see it.

But the real impetus for film soleil was the economic forces in the 1980s, that heightened or made more attractive to filmmakers the already existing elements of noir, economic conditions that have returned with key variations. Most soleils are set in California and the west, the chosen playground and the ideological induction center for Ronald Reagan, whose economic policies created the America that spawned film soleil as a reaction, and now of George W. Bush and his advisors. If the economic climate changes, will soleil continue to be viable? Is it a style vital enough to adapt to change, as few highly specific genres seem to be?

Explicators of noir were quick to find its sociological roots in post war anomie. Some also point out its implicitly rebellious nature, consisting of films going against the grain of normally happy and upbeat Hollywood cinema, by offering up the opposite of John Wayne as its central characters: men who are paranoid, weak, greedy, and ignoble. Some commentators add that, alongside the world of journalism and pulp fiction, these films emerged from an intellect-artistic milieu that included radicals, many of whom were blacklisted.

Film soleil also has its socio-economic aspect. The height of film soleil is the 1990s, in American politics, the Bill Clinton decade. But given the long lead-time inherent in post studio system Hollywood, many of these 1990s film soleil were conceived of in the 1980s or are rooted in the concerns of those who came of age then. In a sense, film soleil's dominance in the 1990s is in defiance of the socio-logical "feel" of the times. Instead the films hark back to what is popularly characterised as the greedy self-interested, anti-populism of the Reagan 1980s. The signature line of the time was that of Gordon Gecko in Oliver Stone's *Wall Street*: "Greed is good. Greed works." As with so many lines of dialogue in movies meant to belittle the times, it instead became a motto.

In the Cyber 'Oughts, the first decade of the century is characterised by isolation, men and women whose primary relationships are with their computers.

The film that sparked film soleil, the Coen Brothers' *Blood Simple*, is emblematic of subsequent film soleil in that none of its successors really resembles it or each other. *After Dark, My Sweet* (1990) and *The Grifters* (1990) explicitly embrace

Thompsonian nihilism. Director Carl Franklin and screen-writers Billy Bob Thornton and Tom Epperson's *One False Move*, which tracks a number of doomed people who congregate in Star City, Arkansas, explores the tensions underlying race relations in America with a Faulkneresque vigor. Tamra Davis' *Guncrazy* (1992) is a quietly hilarious social satire, presenting Drew Barrymore as a 16-year-old living in a desolate trailer with her mom's boyfriend (Joe Dallesandro). Barrymore's boyfriend (James LeGros) is an ex-con with a penchant for guns – which she picks up from him at the expense of her "stepfather," a few local teens and several cops (she then passed it on metaphorically to Mickey and Mallory in *Natural Born Killers,* 1994). Davis and screen-writer Matthew Bright draw on the rich heritage of American road films and criminal couplings to rub the viewer's nose in soured romantic dreams, despite the dire circumstances. *Suture* (1993), the debut feature of co-directing Coenheads Scott McGehee and David Siegel (who went on to make the soleil-ish variation *Deep End*, itself a remake of Ophuls' *The Reckless Moment*), is a body-switching thriller akin to the Frederick Nealy novel that was turned into *Shattered* (Wolfgang Petersen, 1991). *Suture* is a medita-tion of the inability of people to see what is right in front of them, made clear by the Buñuelian casting of the two central characters, two brothers, one white (Michael Harris) and the other black (Dennis Haysbert), a fact upon which no one remarks. This recurring theme of moral blindness plays itself out in the concluding images, in which a shrink intones moralising platitudes about Haysbert and his future, over images that show him living happily ever after.

Among the many directors who have dabbled in film soleil – John Flynn (*Rolling Thunder*), Stephen Frears (*The*

Grifters), Roger Donaldson (*White Sands*, *The Getaway*), Martin Scorsese (*Cape Fear*), Bradley Battersby (*Blue Desert*) – some auteurs have emerged as specialists. Premier among them is John Dahl, all of whose films tend to be soleils. Dahl digs deep into soleil concerns. His output, small though it is, helps codify the elements of the sub-genre – the uncompromisingly selfish woman, the blending of cop and crook roles, and the hero from nowhere with practically no identity. James Foley, it turns out, is another soleil obsessed filmmaker.

Soleil has silently permeated the culture and influenced other movies. Variations on soleil's concerns include: *Wild at Heart* (1990), David Lynch's film from a novel by Barry Gifford, who also wrote a book about film noir; *Thelma & Louise* (1991), a semi-feminist reversal of the traditional road film, drawing upon some elements of film soleil; and *Flesh and Bone* (1993), Steve Kloves' examination of memory and regret, that features practically every element of film soleil except the ineffable patina of an actual crime film (though a crime takes place).

Film soleil is a fairly thriving genre for one few people have identified. Of about 153 noir-style films (listed in an appendix to the third edition of Silver and Ward's *Film Noir: An Encyclopedia Reference to the America Style*) released between 1980 and 1992, 46 – just under a third – have been soleils. Once it is pinned down by critical scrutiny, filmmakers may actually strive to make soleils, as James Foley did with *Confidence*.

Exploration of the genre has been based less on homage to Genres Past than on reactions to America Present. At the same time each individual soleil is more unlike than similar to all the others, a condition that obtains more so here than in any other genre – or style or approach (however one

23

wants to designate soleil). Can a genre survive when the characteristics that join all the members together are so fragile?

Film soleil has its roots in a certain kind of French thriller, of which *Pepe Le Moko* (1937) is perhaps the platonic ideal. As James Naremore describes these French precursors to film noir, they are "shadowy melodramas, set in an urban criminal milieu and featuring doomed protagonists who behaved with sangfroid under pressure." (in *More Than Night*.) Like several of its cousins, *Pepe Le Moko* spotlights a hero who has crossed a racial line; he has gone south and mingled with The Other. As Naremore points out in his book, there was an exploration of racial issues in French film noir at the time which gave the designation "black film" an ambiguous connotation.

One significant difference between film noir and film soleil is that in modern neo-noirs there is that huge body of traditional noirs that filmmakers can find influential or outright reject, or perform variations on. Noir, drawing upon horror films, German expressionism, policiers and other sources, draws disparately from numerous influences. Perhaps that is one reason why noir is so hard to define or pin down as a genre. By the time soleil came along, there were hundreds of noirs of one kind or another, a neo-noir or film soleil director merely had to draw upon noir itself. Thus on the one hand the elements of noir become codified in film soleil, while at the same time the new genre can feel etiolated or desiccated, thanks to the lack of wide ranging influences. Why read books, listen to radio shows, see horror films when all you need do is view 10 or so key noir films?

Thus we have a succession of remakes in which traditional noirs are "turned into" or re-imagined as films soleil: *DOA* is "updated," *Out of the Past* becomes *Against All Odds*. Even an actual soleil such as *The Postman Always Rings Twice* (itself remade in a straightforward manner) is redone again with an Hispanic flavor as *Caught*.

I fret about the fate of film soleil. If directors consciously strive to make films soleils, they could possibly kill off the genre thanks to that self-consciousness – and ultimately the self-parody – that freezes the broad strokes of a genre and drains its life. That would be lamentable, because outside of certain high-profile major Hollywood releases, it is the one form of film that has actually confronted the world, be it race relations (*One False Move*) or economic hazards (*Delusion*) or the unblinkered war between the sexes (*Kalifornia* and most other soleils, in one way or another). The collapse of soleil would simply mark the continued trivialisation of American cinema, in the grip of market researchers and unimaginative corporate robots. Let's hope that young filmmakers stick to their guns and continue to play desert solitaire.

3. A Film Soleil Filmography and Discography

What follows is a chronological account of the films that I've determined to be film soleil, either fully or in embryo. They are arranged year-by-year and then by release date with individual year. Besides a list of *essential* credits, additional information is supplied if the film happens to be available on DVD in Regions 1 and/or 2.

There are anomalies, as there always are in filmographies. For example, although release dates are given, if available, film festival premiere dates are sometimes noted, given that festivals became more important in the 1980s and 1990s, thanks to positive word-of-mouth and the sheer excitement of anticipation these festival debuts inspire. (Finally, key films that epitomise soleil are preceded by a sun icon.)

I intend for this book to be a first approach, not a definitive round up. The catch-all abbreviation that follows, NA, can also mean, "I don't know." For example, my personal film background is weak on Japanese and European films that might qualify as film soleil, and I am eager to learn of such potential titles. One film by a director, say Seijun Suzuki, in some cases serves as a stand-in for a whole host of films I haven't seen yet. Errors and omissions are an inevitable corollary of such tentative baby steps, and I am also happy to entertain suggestions and corrections, via email, at dkholm@mac.com. Corrections will be posted at the blog dedicated to this volume at:

http://homepage.mac.com/dkholm/iblog/B444833512/index.html.

Writing a book on noir and film soleil is a delight. Seeing some of these films for the first time, or even for a third or fourth, thinking about them and reading about them, is continually enriching. Compiling the filmography itself was potentially distracting. Just looking up the cinematographer for, say, *Chinatown*, offered a temptation to stop and simply watch the film again. Ultimately, the designation, film soleil, is also a new excuse to talk about a wealth of beloved films. There are very few truly bad films listed in this filmography, and, as Paul Schrader wrote, "film noir was good for practically every director's career."

In fact, one could copy or revise Andrew Sarris' famous ranking system (used in his book *The American Cinema: Directors and Directions, 1929 – 1968*) based solely on the full range of directors attracted, consciously or not, to soleil. I have taken the liberty of doing so below.

It's fun, yet also painful, to sift through some 200 directors and rank them in order of their ultimate importance. Did Sarris feel a cloud of regret pass across his sun as he consigned the whole career of a director to the dustbin of cinema? Certainly sentimentality plays a role in some high rankings, at least it did for me. And we know a lot more about how films are made these days than did the first readers of Sarris's book (although most of Sarris' rankings remain preternaturally prescient). Directors have written memoirs, revealing who contributed what to their films. Documentaries have profiled some of the greats. Critics such as V. F. Perkins, Robin Wood, Raymond Durgnat, Molly

Haskell, David Bordwell and Kristin Thompson, to name only a few of so many, have taught us to look where we thought there was no more to see. The history of cinema is continuous, evolving, and every new film has the potential to make you rethink all others that came before. In that spirit I offer this ranking as both a shortcut to the specific titles below and as an overall, if tentative, statement of values.

Film Soleil Directors Ranking

The Pantheon

These are the masters, the gods among directors, filmmakers whose careers are now over and whose films have had and will continue to have an everlasting effect on world cinema.

Robert Aldrich   Anthony Mann
Samuel Fuller   Jean-Pierre Melville
Stanley Kubrick   Alan J. Pakula
Sergio Leone   Sam Peckinpah
Louis Malle   Don Siegel

Future Pantheon

Here are working directors who, but for the fact that their careers are still thriving, might well be in the Pantheon. Their films have visual consistency and an individual worldview. When these guys complete or conclude their careers, they will ascent immediately to the Pantheon.

Paul Thomas Anderson   John Boorman
Olivier Assayas   John Carpenter
Peter Bogdanovich   Michael Cimino

Claude Chabrol
Larry Cohen
The Coens
Francis Ford Coppola
John Dahl
Andrew Davis
David Fincher
James Foley
Stephen Frears
William Friedkin
Jonathan Glazer
Jean-Luc Godard
Curtis Hanson
Walter Hill
Mike Hodges
Takeshi Kitano
Steve Kloves
Patrice Leconte
David Lynch
Terrence Malick

James Mangold
Michael Mann
Scott McGehee and David Siegel
John McNaughton
Christopher McQuarrie
John McTiernan
Christopher Nolan
Roman Polanski
Sam Raimi
Francesco Rosi
Martin Scorsese
Paul Schrader
Steven Soderbergh
Steven Spielberg
Quentin Tarantino
Bertrand Tavernier
Paul Verhoeven
Andy and Larry Wachowski
Kar Wai Wong

The Near Side of Paradise

These are the near-greats, filmmakers who have made masterly films, and whose careers still hold potential for greatness, but who, at this point, either have not had a fully fleshed out career or have been hobbled by impediments to their ambition, leaving some of their work compromised by a lack of consistency or other production woes.

George Armitage
Joe Carnahan
D.J. Caruso
Henri-Georges Clouzot

Jules Dassin
Tamra Davis
Brian De Palma
Richard Fleischer

Carl Franklin
Antoine Fuqua
Taylor Hackford
James B. Harris
Neil Jordan
Jonathan Kaplan
Lawrence Kasdan
Joseph Losey
Richard Pearce

Arthur Penn
Bob Rafelson
Karel Reisz
Alan Rudolph
Dominic Sena
Ron Shelton
Oliver Stone
Bob Swaim
Meir Zarchi

Working Stiffs

These are the good, solid dependable directors, whose films can be a pleasure to watch, but whose films don't necessarily demand analysis yet who, on occasion, are capable of making significant cinematic statements.

René Clément
John Flynn
Tay Garnett
Stephen Hopkins
John Irvin
Phil Karlson
Robert Mulligan
Michael Ritchie

Mark Robson
William A. Seiter
Barry Sonnenfeld
John Sturges
Robert Towne
Edgar G. Ulmer
Gore Verbinski
Peter Yates

Cable Ready

Grouped here are mundane directors of no discernable style, theme, or lasting achievement, often because of their lack of ambition, their willingness to compromise with studios, their satisfaction with mere commercialism, or because they are happy to be tools of actors, producers, or studios.

Lewis Allen
Bruce Beresford
Liliana Cavani
Peter Collinson
Delmer Daves
Roger Donaldson
Gordon Douglas
John Herzfeld
Burt Kennedy
George Launtner

Mike Newell
Arthur Ripley, Jr.
Stuart Rosenberg
Jack Smight
John Stahl
Lee Tamahori
Ted Tetzlaff
J. Lee Thompson
Michael Winner

Less than Meets the Eye

The most painful category to assign, these are filmmakers whose reputations far exceed actual achievement, often aided by a beguiling visual style or a consistency of theme that borders on the rigid, and therefore they are easily discernable by the masses and populist critics.

Robert Altman
Hal Ashby
Michael Curtiz
Blake Edwards
Mike Figgis
John Frankenheimer
F. Gary Gray
Phil Joanou
E. Elias Merhige

Tony Richardson
Ridley Scott
Joel Schumacher
Bryan Singer
James Toback
Wayne Wang
Robert Wise
William Wyler

Actors as Directors

Gathered together here are actors seized, for some insane reason, with the itch to control the cinematic product instead of settling for being just another ingredient. What their films often establish in indistinguishable stylistic uniformity they sometimes make up for in earnestness and "edginess".

Robert Culp
Jon Favreau
Dennis Hopper

Sondra Locke
Jack Nicholson
Sean Penn

Subjects for Further Research

These fit into no other category. Oddities, short careers, one hit wonders, or directors whose large filmographies are not as readily available for viewing as some of their peers. This is the category with the greatest potential for future reclassification.

Roy Ward Baker
Bradley Battersby
Jean-Jacques Beineix
Daniel M. Cohen
Peter Collinson
Carl Colpaert
Robinson Devor
David Dobkin
Bruno Dumont
Gary Fleder
Mark Frost
Maggie Greenwald
Brian Koppelman and David Levien
Wayne Kramer
Mary Lambert
Ray Lawrence

Jennifer Leitzes
Ye Lou
John Mackenzie
Jim McBride
Fernando Meirelles and Kátia Lund
Rocky Morton and Annabel Jankel
Michael Oblowitz
Ivan Passer
Mark Reichert
Jean-François Richet
Scott Roberts
Scott Sanders
Bob Swaim
Matthew Warchus

Sun-Bleached Precursors: The Roots of Film Soleil (1942–1959)

1942

Ossessione; *Director:* Luchino Visconti; *Writer:* Visconti, plus Mario Alicata, Giuseppe De Santis, Antonio Pietrangeli, and Gianni Puccini, from the novel *The Postman Always Rings Twice* by James M. Cain; *Key Cast:* Clara Calamai (Giovanna Bragana), Massimo Girotti (Gino Costa), Juan de Landa (Giuseppe Bragana); *Cinematography:* Domenico Scala and Aldo Tonti; *Music:* Giuseppe Rosati; *Studio/Distributor:* ICI; *Running Time:* 140 minutes; *Release Date:* 16 May, 1943, Italy; *Rating:* NR; *DVD: Region 1:* Image, July 2002, 3.33:1; *Region 2:* NA.

Premise: A drifter conspires with a woman to kill her husband

Italian directors start out like Rossellini and end up as Visconti. Even Rossellini and Visconti did. Both began in the so-called neo-realist mode and ended up doing lavish historical dramas. With *Ossessione*, Visconti may not only have contributed a key film in neo-realism, but invented film soleil. On the surface it's a post-war melodrama derived from the Cain novel (which was filmed before, in France in 1939 by Pierre Chenal as *Le Dernier Tournant*). Various censorship and political problems plagued the film in its homeland and, like many masterpieces, its restoration history is convoluted. Visconti's version didn't enjoy release in America until 1976. Like something out of Fellini, there are long dusty roads and decrepit trucks used for multiple purposes, hustlers doing odd shows in town squares, and drifters and sweat and men who are used to traveling. The story is the same as in all the other versions. A drifter named Gino (Massimo Girotti) ends up in a small way station, a lonely diner and gas station in the middle of nowhere, run by a stolid older man (Juan de Landa) and his wife Giovanna (Clara Calamai), who in the past may have been a prostitute. Gino stays on, has an affair, runs away with another fellow (in a barely disguised gay subplot that in fact has tangible links to Cain's work), and participates in the murder of the husband. But although the film begins in a "neo-realist" mode, it becomes more phantasmagoric or stylish as it progresses. While staying much more "realistic" than the Hollywood versions, it also presents the characters less reprehensibly. And like the French new wave films that followed, the film embraces, but not without alteration, film noir and its sources in American popular literature.

1944

✷ *Double Indemnity*; *Director*: Billy Wilder; *Writer*: Wilder, with Raymond Chandler, from a novel by James M. Cain; *Key Cast*: Fred MacMurray (Walter Neff), Barbara Stanwyck (Phyllis Dietrichson), Edward G. Robinson (Barton Keyes); *Cinematography*: John Seitz; *Music*: Miklos Rozsa; *Studio/Distributor:* Paramount; *Running Time*: 107 minutes; *Release Date*: 6 September, 1944, USA; *Rating*: NR; *DVD*: *Region 1*: Image, January 1998, OOP, 1.33:1; *Region 2*: NA.

Premise: An insurance man throws it all away for an attractive woman

At the time, Billy Wilder probably didn't think he was making a film noir. He probably thought he was simply shooting a crime thriller about lust and money, as did most of the directors later categorised as noir practitioners. *Double Indemnity* straddles both noir and soleil; it has the sun-bleached setting, but the classic noir tale. As Neff says, "I killed him for money and for a woman. I didn't get the money and I didn't get the woman," which could summarise many noirs. Wilder's comically ironic tone is like a sickly sheen over his image clusters of trains, tracks, cars, jewelry, phones, money, and liquor.

1945

✻ ***Mildred Pierce***; *Director:* Michael Curtiz; *Writer:* Ranald MacDougall, with William Faulkner and Catherine Turney, from a novel by James M. Cain; *Key Cast:* Joan Crawford (Mildred Pierce Beragon), Jack Carson (Wally Fay), Zachary Scott (Monte Beragon), Ann Blyth (Veda Pierce Forrester); *Cinematography:* Ernest Haller; *Music:* Max Steiner; *Studio/Distributor:* Warner; *Running Time:* 111 minutes; *Release Date:* 20 October, 1945, USA; *Rating:* NR; *DVD:* *Region 1:* Warner, February 2003, 1.33:1, with documentary about Crawford; *Region 2:* NA.

Premise: A career woman does everything on behalf of her ungrateful daughter

Like many a Joan Crawford soaper, *Mildred Pierce* is told in flashback, as if the "present" is too intense, too fragile to bear Crawford's gaunt "now"-ness. The fruit of Crawford's departure from MGM to Warner, the film benefits from collaborators able to bend their talents to the aesthetic demands of this fascinating screen presence. A blend of noir and women's soap opera, it's also a soleil precursor thanks to its pushing the hard edge of familial dissonance: Mildred's daughter is eminently unworthy of her mother's attentions. "With this money," she says, "I can get away from you. From you and your chickens and your pies and your kitchens and everything that smells of grease." Rarely do Hollywood movies of that era dare to suggest that children can be unlikable. With its sun and seaside setting, its diner (acknowledging a newly mobile society like Preminger's *Angel Face*) and its angular "modern" interior it subtly makes a statement about a postwar society in turmoil.

Detour; *Director*: Edgar G. Ulmer; *Writer:* Martin Goldsmith, with Martin Mooney, from a novel by Leon Fromkess; *Key Cast*: Tom Neal (Al Roberts), Ann Savage (Vera); *Cinematography*: Benjamin H. Klein; *Music*: Leo Erdody; *Studio/Distributor:* PRC; *Key Quote*: *Running Time*: 67 minutes; *Release Date*: 30 November, 1945, USA; *Rating*: NR; *DVD*: *Region 1*: Image, September 2000, full frame, Alpha Video, October, 2002, 1.33:1; *Region 2*: NA.

Premise: A musician hitchhikes through the southwest to reach his girlfriend

A key film noir, thanks mostly to its "philosophy" ("That's life. Whichever way you turn, Fate sticks out a foot to trip you,") *Detour* is a terribly acted and mounted film that demands patience and indulgence from the viewer, hence the director, Edgar G. Ulmer, is consequently a test case for auteurism. There had been road films in the 1930s, of course, thanks to the displacements caused by the Depression, but with the advent of film soleil, highways and cars become isolating, terrifying, dangerous things, and forms of communication, such as telephones, become instruments of death, in this grimly absurd case, literally.

Leave Her to Heaven; *Director:* John Stahl; *Writer:* Jo Swerling, from the novel by Ben Ames Williams; *Key Cast:* Gene Tierney (Ellen Berent Harland), Cornel Wilde (Richard Harland), Jeanne Crain (Ruth Berent), Vincent Price (Russell Quinton); *Cinematography:* Leon Shamroy; *Music:* Alfred Newman; *Studio/Distributor:* Fox; *Running Time:* 110 minutes; *Release Date:* 19 December, 1945, USA; *Rating:* NR; *DVD: Region 1:* Fox, February 2005, 1.33:1, with scholar commentary, Movietone News footage, restoration comparison, stills; *Region 2:* NA.

Premise: A woman with an obsessive approach to love marries a novelist

One of a handful of noirs set in the wooded Northern world, *Leave Her to Heaven* is a blend of women's weepie and crime film as well as featuring a lead female character who is insane. Another example is Joan Crawford in *Possessed*. A crafty critic can garner a certain amount of agreeable outrage by asserting sympathy with Tierney's nutty professional wife, who is understood by her family as having obsessively loved her own father. The film is very good at capturing those subtle, unstated family tensions that outsiders barge in on unwittingly and fail to weigh accurately. By seeing Ellen's side of the story, so to speak, the critic or viewer is establishing an insightful contrariness that goes against the grain of common Hollywood audience sense. In the real world we tend to be, or have had fits of being, more like Ellen than the bland characters for whom she is competing. Subversively, Ellen is the real heroine. Her ruthlessness, single-mindedness, and craftiness, even beyond death, would certainly become virtues in the action and siege movies of the 1980s and 1990s, and her mere presence highlights the absolute narcissism of her family.

1946

❋ *The Postman Always Rings Twice*; *Director:* Tay Garnett; *Writer:* Harry Ruskin, with Niven Busch, from a novel by James M. Cain; *Key Cast:* John Garfield (Frank Chambers), Lana Turner (Cora Smith), Cecil Kellaway (Nick Smith); *Cinematography:* Sidney Wagner; *Music:* George Bassman, with Eric Zeisl; *Studio/Distributor:* MGM; *Running Time:* 113 minutes; *Release Date:* 2 May, 1946, USA; *Rating:* NR; *DVD:* *Region 1:* Warner, January 2004, 1.33:1, with documentary on Garfield, introduction by Richard Jewell, stills; *Region 2:* NA.

Premise: A drifter comes between a husband and wife

Like Herman Melville's white whale, Cain and Turner's Cora is the surprising equivalent of danger. But unlike the common image of the femme fatale in other noirs, Cora isn't necessarily evil. Misguided, maybe, and consumed by lust, but not downright evil (did contemporary audiences understand this?). Cora and Frank fall into murder as if by a series of logical, tumbling locks. The first official film based on Cain's novel, this *Postman* is very much a film soleil, having few of the visual cues of traditional noir. Like many noirs, it is really a soap opera. Like many soleil, it is really ironical.

1947

Riffraff; *Director*: Ted Tetzlaff; *Writer:* Martin Rackin; *Key Cast*: Pat O'Brien (Dan Hammer), Anne Jeffreys (Maxine Manning), Walter Slezak (Eric Molinar); *Cinematography*: George E. Diskant; *Music*: Roy Webb and Joan Whitney; *Studio/Distributor:* RKO; *Running Time*: 80 minutes; *Release Date*: 15 September, 1947, USA; *Rating*: NR; *DVD*: NA.

Premise: A private eye in Mexico comes between various spies and thieves

A film soleil thanks to its Latin American setting (increasingly common from the late 1930s on), this is a crime tale from the Hollywood tough guy school, with *To Have and Have Not* probably another commercial influence, although O'Brien's PI act is hollow and false. From its Hammett-esque beatings to its fey villain filling in sketchbooks, the film tends to be theatrical rather than felt, probably due in large part to its stage-bound settings. Anne Jeffreys, however, is a revelation as the Hawksian chanteuse who has been down too many roads to be taken in by O'Brien's artifice.

❋ *Out of the Past*; *Director*: Jacques Tourneur; *Writer:* Geoffrey Homes (Daniel Mainwaring), Frank Fenton and James M. Cain, from a novel by Homes; *Key Cast*: Robert Mitchum (Jeff Bailey), Jane Greer (Kathie Moffat), Kirk Douglas (Whit Sterling), Rhonda Fleming (Meta Carson); *Cinematography*: Nicholas Musuraca; *Music*: Roy Webb;

Studio/Distributor: RKO; *Running Time:* 97 minutes; *Release Date:* 13 November, 1947, US; *Rating:* NR; *DVD: Region 1:* Warner Video, July 2004, 3.33:1, with critic audio commentary, trailers; *Region 2:* NA.

Premise: A former PI on the run recounts the case and the woman who drove him underground

A Whitman sampler of noir variations, *Out of the Past* is one part fatalistic noir, one part melodrama, one part Hammet-like hardboiled, detective story (the San Francisco sequence), one part soap opera, one part woodsy melodrama (like *Leave Her to Heaven*), and one part film soleil, thanks to its Mexico sequence. It's a multi-layered tale with an interesting internal symmetry whose key bit of dialogue is, "Baby, I don't care." For a quintessential noir, it's funny how un-noirish it is. With the novelistic device of multiple flashbacks, it's also told in a series of long Mitchum-drawled voice-overs. It's also a rich film that rewards multiple viewings, as it seems to contain *all* cinema.

1948

✱ *The Lady from Shanghai*; *Director:* Orson Welles; *Writer:* Orson Welles, with William Castle, Charles Lederer, and Fletcher Markle, from a novel by Sherwood King; *Key Cast:* Orson Welles (Michael O'Hara), Rita Hayworth (Elsa Bannister), Everett Sloan (Arthur Bannister), Glenn Anders (George Grisby); *Cinematography:* Charles Lawton, Jr., with Rudolph Mate and Joseph Walker; *Music:* Heinz Roemheld; *Studio/Distributor:* Columbia; *Running Time:* 87 minutes; *Release Date:* 9 June, 1948, USA; *Rating:* NR; *DVD: Region 1:* Columbia-Tristar, October 2000, 1.33:1, with commentary by Peter Bogdanovich; *Region 2*: NA. Note: The film was released much later after its completion.

Premise: A drifter comes between a husband and wife and their hangers on

With *Citizen Kane*, Welles could be said to invent noir; with *The Lady from Shanghai*, he helped invent film soleil. It's not just the sunny setting, but also the murder for hire, also found later in *Kill Me Again* and the nightmare like visuals that suggest that in this world anything goes. The plot defies summary, but is coherent. *Lady's* release was delayed in the US until 1948, so its influence on other films was delayed, but once it kicks in, the influence is pervasive, later compounded by *Touch of Evil*. Its image clusters of sea, sand, ships, and subterfuge add up to a tumultuous tale of Rococo 'fatedness' – for all its secondary characters.

1949

❋ *Thieves' Highway* [*Collision*]; *Director*: Jules Dassin; *Writer*: A. I. Bezzerides, from his novel; *Key Cast*: Richard Conte (Nico Garcos), Valentina Cortesa (Rica), Lee J. Cobb (Mike Figlia), Barbara Lawrence (Polly Faber); *Cinematography*: Norbert Brodine; *Music*: Alfred Newman; *Studio/Distributor*: Fox; *Running Time*: 94 minutes; *Release Date*: 10 October, 1949, USA; *Rating*: NR; *DVD*: *Region 1*: Criterion, February 2005, 1.33:1, with audio commentary by Alain Silver, video interview with Dassin, trailer, writer profile; *Region 2*: NA.

Premise: A returning vet seeks to redeem his trucker father Richard Conte is now, sadly, a little recognised B-movie action star, a poor man's John Garfield, an ethnic street tough with a soft heart, a powerhouse guy you'd prefer not to cross. He was great as the innocent man in *Northside 777*, and was such an influence or hero to filmmakers that one of them, Scorsese, for example, borrowed Conte's catch phrase, "*Now is the time*," from his Korean war film *Target Zero* (Harmon Jones, 1955) for the end of *Mean Streets*. Here he enjoys one of his premiere roles. Another one of those noir variations that make it hard to define the genre, it is set in the workaday world, but it is also a road film, and much of it takes place in daylight. It's got a bit of the "returning vet" premise going, but its noir bleakness is undermined by what is more or less an imposed happy ending. In fact it has more in common with the proletarian crime dramas Warners did in the 1930s. Its critique of capitalism is also important. The narrative doesn't follow the track you expect, and there is weird tension in the film. It makes you itchy and uncomfortable. This makes it one of the most interesting noirs, because it is not what we expect, and the tension becomes mysterious and unique.

✻ ***Border Incident***; *Director:* Anthony Mann; *Writer:* John C. Higgins, with George Zuckerman; *Key Cast:* Ricardo Montalban (Pablo Rodriguez), George Murphy (Jack Bearnes), Howard Da Silva (Owen Parkson); *Cinematography:* John Alton; *Music:* Andre Previn; *Studio/Distributor:* MGM; *Running Time:* 94 minutes; *Release Date:* 28 October 1949, USA; *Rating:* NA; *DVD:* NA.

Premise: Federal agents crack an illegal immigration operation

A blend of the brightness found in the semi–documentary

post war noirs and the inky blackness indigenous to Anthony Mann's films, *Border Incident* is a key early harbinger of film soleil, with its southwestern setting, its border farm, and its ambiguous stance toward crime. Notable enough to inspire a rank imitator (see the following year's *Borderline*), *Border Incident* is also unabashed in its portrayal of the villain's ruthlessness, and in one key scene an undercover agent is murdered while his partner watches helplessly in secret nearby. Mann is so heralded as a visual director that critics are apt to forget that he elicited astounding performances from his casts (especially in the James Stewart westerns). Here, far from top of the line journeymen, such as George Murphy and Ricardo Montalban offer, up perhaps their peak performances.

1950

Borderline; *Director*: William A. Seiter; *Writer*: Devery Freeman; *Key Cast*: Fred MacMurray (Johnny McEvoy), Claire Trevor (Madeleine Haley), Raymond Burr (Pete Ritchie); *Cinematography*: Lucien Andriot; *Music*: Hans J. Salter; *Studio/Distributor*: Universal; *Running Time*: 88 minutes; *Release Date*: 1 March, 1950, USA; *Rating*: NR; *DVD*: *Region 1*: Brentwood, July 2004, 1.33:1; *Region 2*: NA.

Premise: Two agents unknowingly infiltrate a smuggling operation at the same time

The flat, elusive title *Borderline* promises a lot; and in the hands of, say, Anthony Mann, the film might have delivered. However, Seiter's film is a reminder of noir's roots in B films while at the same time undermining interest in its conventional story by failing to capitalise on its few virtues of casting and concept, or transcending its limitations in an Ulmerian manner. It is set in the charged ambiguity and moral bankruptcy of a border town between Mexico and the United States where all the interiors are shabby sets and the few exteriors have the easily identifiable sunlit quality of Southern California. The film is really about the heroine's eager girl detective adventures, even as the story itself descends into a weird form of sexual chaos, as middlebrow morality grapples with the script's licentious situation, boy and girl on the road together, which has been a staple of Hollywood at least as far back as *It Happened One Night*. Although really a "woman's picture," *Borderline* qualifies as a brief breeze announcing film soleil's mighty wind.

Sunset Blvd.; *Director:* Billy Wilder; *Writer:* Wilder, with Charles Brackett and D. M. Marshman Jr.; *Key Cast:* William Holden (Joe Gillis), Gloria Swanson (Norma Desmond), Erich von Stroheim (Max von Mayerling), Nancy Olson (Betty Schaefer); *Cinematography:* John F. Seitz; *Music:* Franz Waxman; *Studio/Distributor:* Paramount; *Running Time:* 110 minutes; *Release Date:* 4 August 1950, USA; *Rating:* NR; *DVD:* *Region 1:* Paramount, November 2002, 1.33:1, with critic commentary, making ofs, maps, gallery, and prologue assembly; *Region 2:* NA.

Premise: A failed screenwriter takes haven in a fading silent star's estate

One of the most written about movies, *Sunset Blvd.* is widely considered the best film about Hollywood. But for true connoisseurs, it is the model for all other Billy Wilder films; for advocates of film soleil it also shows that soleil-esque properties can exist in the most un-noir-like context, for William Holden as Joe Gillis is perhaps the premiere film soleil man. A hustler. Not too bright. A guy able to see the main chance and go for it. But with enough integrity to make him sick with himself for stringing along an aging silent screen star, "working" on her screenplay, and sleeping with her just to live the life of Riley for a while (the "ageing" star played by Gloria Swanson was, by the way, simply in her early 40s). One thing little remarked upon about *Sunset Blvd.*, however, is how *literary* it is. Wilder and Brackett's script employs an elaborate flashback device. It also breaks the fourth way by first using main character narration but also having this monologue emerge from the mouth of a dead guy. And in its romantic somberness about lost glory and the sadness of growing old it embraces the sort of twilight ideas found in film soleil.

1951

❋ *Ace in the Hole* [*The Big Carnival*]; *Director*: Billy Wilder; *Writer*: Wilder, with Walter Newman and Lesser Samuels; *Key Cast*: Kirk Douglas (Charles Tatum), Jan Sterling (Lorraine Minosa); *Cinematography*: Charles B. Lang, Jr.; *Music*: Hugo Friedhofer; *Studio/Distributor*: Paramount; *Running Time*: 111 minutes; *Release Date*: 29 June, 1951, USA; *Rating*: NR; *DVD*: NA.

Premise: An unscrupulous journalist exploits an unfolding tragedy

The bedrock cynicism of this Billy Wilder film, his first made

outside the sphere of his arranged marriage to writer partner
Charles Brackett, perhaps distracted contemporary viewers
from its mordant social commentary and media criticism
("It's a good story today. Tomorrow, they'll wrap a fish in it")
and made it an easy target for dismissive reviewers.
Unfortunately, reputedly bad box office and flailing title
changes assured that the film failed to attract viewers and
indeed it may have temporarily damaged Wilder's career
(always shaky, given that he was a writer – that despised
breed – turned director). Today it is commonplace to note
that this holds up as good if not better than many of the
surrounding Wilder titles. It is entirely consistent with
Wilder's other films, which usually profiled a hustler playing
the suckers on his way to (Hollywood imposed?) redemp-
tion. Wilder here uses the blistering sun well as a stand-in for
a cruel God judging earthlings. Douglas' journalist, a throw-
back to and updating of the dipsomaniacal scribes of 1930s
screwball, has the selfish drive of all soleil anti-heroes.

1952

Kansas City Confidential; *Director*: Phil Karlson; *Writer*:
Karlson, with Rowland Brown, George Bruce, Harry Essex,
Harold R. Greene, and John Payne; *Key Cast*: John Payne
(Joe Rolfe/Peter Harris), Coleen Gray (Helen Foster aka
Punkin), Preston Foster (Tim Foster); *Cinematography*:
George E. Diskant; *Music*: Paul Sawtell; *Studio/Distributor*:
UA; *Running Time*: 99 minutes; *Release Date*: 28 November,
1952, USA; *Rating*: NA; *DVD*: *Region 1*: Image, June 2004,
1.33:1, bios, star interview, stills, trailer for *5 Against the
House*; *Region 2*: NA.

Premise: A man framed for an armored car robbery seeks out those who did it

Phil Karlson specialised in the ironies of film noir fate, like a cinematic Cornell Woolrich. The interesting thing about *Kansas City Confidential* is that, as Alain Silver points out in the indispensable *Film Noir* encyclopedia, the hazards of fate and coincidence are doubled. The protagonist is an innocent bystander who just happened to be driving a truck the gang needed to employ. But then, as a freewheeling unknown agent, he ends up playing a major part in the fate of the gang members. As far as soleil goes, however, Karlson wouldn't know how to shoot a daylight scene if he had to, and although some of the film takes place in Mexico, he prefers the night, with its heat, its smoke, and its shadows. He is also fond of close ups, for they tend to make us identify with the characters, even the bad guys. The film works numerous changes on its small-scale crew of characters and situations, and the whole cast is excellent.

1953

✳ *The Wages of Fear* [*Le Salaire de la peur*]; *Director:* Henri-Georges Clouzot; *Writer:* Clouzot, with Jérome Geronimi from the novel by Georges Arnaud; *Key Cast:*Yves Montand (Mario), Charles Vanel (M. Jo), Peter Van Eyck (Bimba); *Cinematography:* Armand Thirard; *Music:* Georges Auric; *Studio/Distributor:* Cinedis; *Running Time:* 83 minutes; *Release Date:* 22 April, 1953, France; *Rating:* NR; *DVD: Region 1:* Criterion, February 1999, 1.33:1, uncensored version; *Region 2:* NA.

Premise: Four exiles in a Latin American country take one last chance to get out

Rarely has French existential angst found its most perfect realisation. The seeming futility of the men's task (driving dynamite to a flaming oil well), its surprising success, and then the absurdity of the lone survivor's capricious demise, suggest a darkening at odds with the brilliance of the film's setting, a Latin American country to which the quartet are self-exiled. The impact of the film must have been much greater upon release, when happy endings were still conventional. Yet today the film still has the power to inspire hope, depression, and doubt.

❋ *Inferno*; *Director:* Roy Ward Baker; *Writer:* Francis M. Cockwell; *Key Cast:* Robert Ryan (Donald Whitley Carson III), Rhonda Fleming (Geraldine Carson), William Lundigan (Joseph Duncan); *Cinematography*: Lucien Ballard; *Music:* Paul Sawtell; *Studio/Distributor:* Fox; *Running Time*: 83 minutes; *Release Date*: 12 August, 1953, USA; *Rating*: NR; *DVD*: NA.

Premise: A wounded millionaire is abandoned to the desert by his calculating wife

Inferno is a great "little" film, an unpretentious psychological drama about survival, as well as a bleak examination of American marriage. It also continues 1950s' American cinema's strange fascination with the desert, be it for the birthplace of monsters or the setting for psychodrama. Robert Ryan is in rare heroic mode as the abandoned husband who must fight to live, and Rhonda Fleming is strangely sexy as his harridan of a scheming wife. It's like a *Postman Always Rings Twice* told from the viewpoint of the husband–victim. In what could have been a rather detached, mostly visual film, the filmmakers have chosen to include a voice-over of the husband's thoughts, but the film's vigorous B-action muscle makes up for this concession to the obvious. Ryan's husband is a compromised hero, a selfish tycoon who has to earn the viewer's respect. Perhaps the optimum soleil of the 1950s, *Inferno* suggests depths to the otherwise under-appreciated career of director Baker, who has gone from British thrillers to Monroe vehicles to disaster films (*A Night to Remember*) to episodes of *The Avengers*, to one of the better Quatermass films to horror and finally to episodic TV. *Inferno* deserves to be on DVD – which poses a problem as the film was originally released in wide screen 3D. All too often plot points must be bent in order to accommodate the actualisation of trick effects, but the film's "interiority" transcends its purely commercial ambitions.

1955

✳ **Bad Day at Black Rock**; *Director*: John Sturges; *Writer*: Don McGuire and Millard Kaufman, from a short story by Howard Breslin; *Key Cast*: Spencer Tracy (John J. Macreedy), Robert Ryan (Reno Smith), Anne Francis (Liz Wirth), Dean Jagger (Sheriff Tim Horn), Ernest Borgnine (Coley Trimble), Lee Marvin (Hector David); *Cinematography*: William C. Mellor; *Music*: Andre Previn; *Studio/Distributor*: MGM; *Running Time*: 81 minutes; *Release Date*: 7 January, 1955, USA; *Rating*: NR; *DVD*: *Region 1*: Warner, May 2005, 2.40:1, with audio commentary by Dana Polan; *Region 2*: NA. Note:

The old Criterion laserdisc has an audio commentary track by John Sturges that is considered one of the best.

Premise: A stranger disrupts a small, corrupt town

A decade on, American cinema was still dealing with the war years, the home front, and the uneasy remerging of vet and society (though this film is set just after the war). A B-action version of the *Best Years of Our Lives*, *Bad Day* is an efficient if slow paced and stripped down thriller that blends tangents of the western with some noir concerns and a social conscience about xenophobia. The film might have been better if director Sturges had slowed events down even further, to a Sergio Leone pace, with the commensurate visual sophistication (Leone, for example, would not have filled a static place with all manner of vehicles such as jeeps and trains). As it stands *Bad Day* is of more sociological than cinematic importance, but historically it does have a role as an early film soleil.

Kiss Me Deadly [*Mickey Spillane's Kiss Me Deadly*]; *Director:* Robert Aldrich; *Writer:* Harry Kleiner and Fuller; *Key Cast:* Ralph Meeker (Mike Hammer), Albert Dekker (Dr. G.E. Soberin), Maxine Cooper (Velda), Cloris Leachman (Christina Bailey), Gaby Rodgers (Lily Carver); *Cinematography*: Ernest Laszlo; *Music*: Frank DeVol; *Studio/Distributor:* UA; *Running Time*: 106 minutes; *Release Date*: 18 May, 1955, USA; *Rating*: NR; *DVD*: Region 1: MGM, June 2001, 1.66:1, with alternate ending; *Region 2*: NA.

Premise: PI Mike Hammer investigates a murder that he wasn't able to prevent

Along with *Touch of Evil* this is the quintessential 1950s noir, esteemed by critics because it is also a critique of 1950s society (red-baiting, the A-bomb) and a subversive undermining of Mickey Spillane's source novel. It is a great film, and the transition of the setting from New York to Los Angeles slides it in the film soleil direction. Aldrich has "intellectualised" components of the story and rendered Meeker's Hammer a blundering bull in the cultural china shop. What is remarkable about the film within the context of Aldrich's other films is that it is more in league with his "women's" pictures (*What Ever Happened to Baby Jane?*, *The Legend of Lylah Clare*) than the manly actioners (*The Dirty Dozen*). The hierarchies of society Hammer travels through are represented by more women than men, who outdo the men in both morality and evil.

❋ *House of Bamboo*; *Director*: Samuel Fuller; *Writer:* Harry Kleiner and Fuller; *Key Cast*: Robert Ryan (Sandy Dawson), Robert Stack (Eddie Kenner/Spanier), Cameron Mitchell (Griff), Brad Dexter (Capt. Hanson); *Cinematography*: Joe McDonald; *Music*: Leigh Harline; *Studio/Distributor:* Fox; *Running Time*: 102 minutes; *Release Date*: 1 July, 1955, USA; *Rating*: NR; *DVD*: *Region 1*: Fox, June 2005, 2.35:1, with critic audio commentary; *Region 2*: NA.

Premise: In post-war Japan, a military cop infiltrates a band of American gangsters

As in *Kiss Me Deadly*, a brute bashes his way through a society he doesn't understand. And as with the famous anecdote about *Ben Hur*, one of the two leads was informed about the homosexual undercurrents of the central friendship and the other wasn't (see the film *The Celluloid Closet* [Rob Epstein, 1995], for the details on the *Ben Hur* case). Here, Ryan collaborated with Fuller on the gay subtext, while Stack was left in the dark. Ryan's character, clearly in love with Stack's character, is solicitous toward him, covetous of his loyalty, and willing to throw over a previous pet for the new guy (this partially anticipates the way De Niro runs his crew in *Heat*). A remake of the *Street With No Name* (William Keighley, 1948), the film is an example of the undercover agent tangent of film noir, and Fuller pretends that we don't know Stack's real purpose for the first 20 minutes or so. The film is sharply written, efficiently shot, and brilliantly acted, especially by Ryan, one of the key players in 1950s soleil.

1956

✸ *The Killing*; *Director:* Stanley Kubrick; *Writer:* Kubrick with Jim Thompson, from a novel by Lionel White; *Key Cast:* Sterling Hayden (Johnny Clay), Coleen Gray (Fay), Vince Edwards (Val Cannon), Elisha Cook (George Peatty), Marie Windsor (Sherry Peatty); *Cinematography:* Lucien Ballard; *Music:* Gerald Fried; *Studio/Distributor:* UA; *Running Time:* 85 minutes; *Release Date:* 6 June, 1956, USA; *Rating:* NR; *DVD: Region 1:* MGM, October 2000, 1.33:1, with trailer; *Region 2:* NA. Note: The Criterion laserdisc of this film is collectable.

Premise: A disparate team attempts a racetack heist

If Stanley Kubrick were looking for a mentor, then he was better off with Max Ophuls, who influenced his later films, than John Huston, who influenced this early feature.

Sentimentality probably plays a part in rendering this one of Kubrick's most overrated films: sentimentality over the passing of traditional noir, and over the host of B–actors who make up the cast. Its mix of documentary realism and noir lighting and stagey theatricality is uneasy, and swallows up the innovations, such as the influential time disruptions. In the end, the "Huston" parts of the film are cold, contrived, and unfelt while the "Ophuls" parts are moving and visually intriguing. Given Thompson's influence on film soleil in general, it's a fun game to figure out Thompson's fingerprints on the finished film, which most likely consists of the brittle, imbalanced marriage of Elisha Cook and Marie Windsor. Overall, the film is really about loyalty and friendship, and Windsor's character is the one who disrupts the loyalty of all the others. Curiously, Kubrick was always very good with scenes of bureaucracy, clerks at counters and the like, and the roots of later great scenes of this kind, always superbly acted, are first seen at the end of the *Killing*.

1958

❋ *Touch of Evil*; *Director*: Orson Welles; *Writer*: Welles, with Paul Monash and Franklin Coen, from a novel by Whit Masterson (Robert Wade and William Miller); *Key Cast*: Orson Welles (Hank Quinlan), Charlton Heston (Ramon Miguel Vargas), Janet Leigh (Susan Vargas), Joseph Calleia (Pete Menzies); *Cinematography*: Russell Metty; *Music*: Henry Mancini; *Studio/Distributor*: Universal; *Running Time*: 95 minutes; *Release Date*: 23 April, 1958, USA; *Rating*: NR; *DVD*: *Region 1*: Universal, October 2000, 1.85:1, with Welles memo to Universal; *Region 2*: NA. Note: There are several versions of the movie; this DVD is the 1998 restoration by

Walter Murch following Welles' notes. A documentary about the making of the film, *Reconstructing Evil*, summarises its production history.

Premise: An idealistic Mexican cop bucks up against his corrupt American counterpart

Having, to some minds, started film noir with *Citizen Kane*, Orson Welles, to some minds, ends it with this policier. Hysterical, unrestrained, personal, it's a film that carries the viewer along with its intensity while painting broad plot points, as in a Sergio Leone film. Its operatic nature makes for big emotions, balanced by quieter, sadder moments stitched into the film's corners. "All border towns bring out the worst in a country," says one of the characters and that could be the anthem for a certain strand of film soleil that *Touch of Evil* represents.

Additional, Potential, or Honorary Films Soleils: 1947: *The Red House*; 1953: *Pickup on South Street*; 1954: *Suddenly*; 1955: *The Desperate Hours, 5 Against the House*; 1956: *The Harder They Fall*; 1958: *Bob Le Flambeur, Thunder Road*; 1959: *The Crimson Kimono, Odds Against Tomorrow; 1937: Pépé le Moko; 1941: High Sierra; 1948: The Treasure of the Sierra Madre.*

Early Film Soleil: The 1960s

With the unofficial death of noir falling in the late 1950s, technological changes in the way films were made, the encroaching importance of television, the collapse of the studio system, and social-political changes in the country, created the groundwork for film soleil to begin to make its presence known.

1960

❋ *Purple Noon* [*Plein soleil*]; *Director:* René Clément; *Writer:* Clément and Paul Gegauff, from the novel *The Talented Mr. Ripley* by Patricia Highsmith; *Key Cast:* Alain Delon (Tom Ripley), Maurice Ronet (Philippe Greenleaf); *Cinematography:* Henri Decaë; *Music:* Nino Rotta (aka Nino Rota); *Studio/Distributor:* Titanus. *Running Time:* 112 minutes; *Release Date:* 10 March 1960, France; *Rating:* PG-13; *DVD:* *Region 1:* Miramax, January 2003, 1.66:1; *Region 2:* Kinowelt, November 2000, 1.78:1, with director interview, stills.

Premise: A wastrel inveigles his way into the life of a rich kid

A textbook film soleil, this adaptation of Highsmith's creepy, subtle novel is near perfect but for the imposed ending in which mainstream justice prevails over crime. Delon is excellent as the opaque hero, whose surface shallowness (and physical beauty) masks a great depth and determination. We never see the mind working, as we do in subsequent Ripley adaptations. In classic soleil manner, the sun beats down mercilessly on the good and the bad, who are hard to tell apart in the context of a new "morality" that abandons 1950s conventionality.

1961

Underworld USA; *Director:* Samuel Fuller; *Writer:* Fuller; *Key Cast:* Cliff Robertson (Tolly Devlin), Dolores Dorn (Cuddles); *Cinematography:* Hal Mohr; *Music:* Harry Sukman; *Studio/Distributor:* Columbia; *Running Time:* 99 minutes; *Release Date:* 13 May, 1961, USA; *Rating:* NR; *DVD:* NA.

Premise: A man takes revenge on the gangsters who killed his dad 20 years earlier

As usual, Fuller here takes a rather conventional story and twists it into a intense, relentless drama and a harsh, unforgiving document about social ills, in this case disparities in economic status, the failure of the justice system, and the psychology of revenge. In fact, *Underworld USA* can be viewed as a variation on the Batman mythos, with Robertson's troubled hero the dark equivalent of Bruce Wayne. In this regard the movie anticipates the darkened palette of subsequent revisionist Batman graphic novels and movies in the 1980s.

1962

❋ *Salvatore Giuliano*; *Director:* Francesco Rosi; *Writer:* Rosi, with Suso Cecchi d'Amico, Enzo Provenzale, and Franco Solinas; *Key Cast:* Pietro Cammarata (Salvatore Giuliano), Gaspare Pisciotta (Frank Wolff); *Cinematography:* Gianni Di Venanzo; *Music:* Piero Piccioni; *Studio/Distributor:* Galatea Film. *Running Time:* 125 minutes; *Release Date:* 28 February 1962, USA; *Rating:* NA; *DVD:* *Region 1:* Criterion, February 2004, 2.35:1/1.33:1/1.85:1, with scholar commentary, newsreels, director interviews, profiles; *Region 2:* NA.

Premise: A chronicle of the post war Mafia rebel

Communication, or the lack of it, is the theme of Rosi's film about the Sicilian bandit who was assassinated, it appears, by a coalition of Mafia chiefs, cops, and politicians in 1950. It's hard to describe the effect of *Salvatore Giuliano* but it is almost magical. It's an oblique film, telling its story of a bandit's last days from a distance. For example, we never really see Giuliano except as a man in a white coat leading a team of mountain men or as a corpse lying in various forums. The focus of the second half of the film becomes his top lieutenant, Gaspare Pisciotta, played by Frank Wolff, an actor very popular with Italian directors. If the first half of the film is about the hills, the second half is about the city, where Pisciotta and numerous other gangsters are on trial. Here the film discreetly tries to account for Giuliano's death. This, too, is typical of director Rosi, whose films take on political subjects, usually conspiracies of one sort or another, but without bombast or dogmatism. *Salvatore Giuliano* influenced contemporary cinema: *The Battle of Algiers, The Godfather, Raging Bull* numerous others. By the way, the Criterion DVD has one of the best audio commentary tracks – by Peter Cowie – ever recorded.

Cape Fear; *Director:* J. Lee Thompson; *Writer:* James R. Webb, from a novel by John D. MacDonald; *Key Cast:* Gregory Peck (Sam Bowden), Robert Mitchum (Max Cady), Polly Bergen (Peggy Bowden); *Cinematography:* Samuel Leavitt; *Music:* Bernard Herrmann; *Studio/Distributor:* Universal; *Running Time:* 105 minutes; *Release Date:* 18 April, 1962, USA; *Rating:* NR; *DVD: Region 1:* Universal, September 2001, 1.85:1, with making of, poster gallery; *Region 2:* NA.

Premise: An ex-con terrorises a family

Orson Welles once said that Bernard Herrmann's music "made" *Citizen Kane*, and that may be true of every film that the composer worked on. It's especially true of this family thriller, which is otherwise visually mundane. Only Martin Scorsese's later re-make captured, unintentionally no doubt, some of the tensions and social observation of John D. MacDonald's source book, a writer under-appreciated for his use of adjectives as moral comments. Like *The Desperate Hours*, the film preys on middle class fear of invasion – by criminals, by chaos, by The Other: whichever you want to call it – post war American cinema is preoccupied by mass invasion and home invasion. In his cunning and ability to anticipate, Max Cady anticipates both the killers in 1970s teen slasher films and Hannibal Lecter.

1963

✹ ***Contempt*** [*Le Mepris*]; *Director*: Jean-Luc Godard; *Writer:* Godard, from the novel by Alberto Moravia; *Key Cast*: Brigitte Bardot (Camille Javal), Michel Piccoli (Paul Javal), Jack Palance (Jeremy Prokosch), Fritz Lang (himself); *Cinematography*: Raoul Coutard; *Music*: Georges Delerue; *Studio/Distributor:* Embassy; *Running Time*: 102 minutes; *Release Date*: 20 December, 1963, France; *Rating*: NR; *DVD*: *Region 1*: Criterion, December 2002, 2.35:1, with scholar commentary, video interview, short film about Lang, contemporaneous making ofs, Godard TV interview, Coutard interview; *Region 2*: Pioneer, April 1999, with reviews.

Premise: A screenwriter contrives to have his wife butter up a movie producer

Critics, simply put, make the best directors. Some of the most intelligent filmmakers in the history of cinema began as critics, among them François Truffaut, Paul Schrader, Claude

Chabrol, Eric Rohmer, Bertrand Tavernier, and Peter Bogdanovich. Many screenwriters, including Paul D. Zimmerman, Frank S. Nugent, and Richard LaGravenese, also began as reviewers. A critic-turned-filmmaker such as Jean-Luc Godard can draw upon pulp novels as the basis for his films without a hint of slumming. In *Sight and Sound*, Colin MacCabe called *Contempt* "the greatest work of art produced in post-war Europe," because of its mixture of modernity with classicism, its poignant use of four languages, and its constant, breathtaking visual beauty. Like all great works of art, *Contempt* is about many things at once. It chronicles the disintegration of a marriage. It portrays prostitution as a metaphor for life in capitalist society. It makes a statement about how movies are made. It is a contemplation of the soul of cinema and the role of the filmmaker in society, and a meditation on two approaches to life, essentially modernity versus antiquity. *Contempt* qualifies as a film soleil, aside from the obviousness of its setting, thanks to its violent end and the blend of ambition and self-loathing in the main character which drives him to, essentially, pimp his wife.

1964

❋ *The Killers*; *Director*: Don Siegel; *Writer:* Gene L. Coon, from a story by Ernest Hemingway; *Key Cast*: Lee Marvin (Charlie Strom), Angie Dickinson (Sheila Farr), John Cassavetes (Johnny North), Clu Gulager (Lee), Ronald Reagan (Jack Browning); *Cinematography*: Richard L. Rawlings; *Music*: Johnny Williams; *Studio/Distributor*: Universal; *Running Time*: 93 minutes; *Release Date*: 7 July, 1964, USA; *Rating*: NR; *DVD*: *Region 1*: Criterion, February 2003, 1.33:1, doubled with Siodmak's *The Killers*, and with video interview with Stuart M. Kaminsky, Screen Director's Playhouse 1949 radio adaptation, starring Burt Lancaster and Shelley Winters, Hemingway story read by Stacy Keach, Paul Schrader's 1972 essay "Notes on Film Noir," music and effects track, video interview with Clu Gulager, excerpts from Don Siegel's autobiography, production correspondence including memos, broadcast standard reports, and casting suggestions, stills, essays by Geoffrey O'Brien, Jonathan Lethem; *Region 2*: NA.

Premise: Hired gunmen relentlessly pursue the fruits of a heist

"There's only one guy who's not afraid to die; that's a guy who's already dead," says Lee Marvin's killer in this film that began as a TV movie and ended up as a future president's last theatrical film. Marvin's killer is bugged by the acceptance of his victim, and that motivates the rest of the movie, with Marvin in essence turning on his employers. The detective in this film, then, is the killer, the usual object of a detective's hunt. What better contrast between classic film noir and film soleil could one find than between the old Robert Siodmak adaptation of Hemingway's story and the modern one? Siodmak's film came at a transitional moment in the history of noir, signaling a transition away from gangsters and toward existential crime thrillers. Siegel's version marks yet another transition, back to the gangster film but in an existential soleil context. As Jack Shadoian points out in his book *Dreams and Dead Ends*, the 1946 version takes on a bleak tone unknown in both noir or gangster films, a world in which corporate American is just as much a hazard to gangsters as the cops. Siodmak's version isn't a great film in the conventional sense, but it is a great noir, and if Siegel's is the lesser movie it is not solely because of its made-for-TV limitations, but because American filmmakers had not figured out how to fully make the transition from black and white noir films to the bright severities of soleil.

1965

✻ *Faster Pussycat! Kill! Kill!* [*The Leather Girls, The Mankillers*]; *Director:* Russ Meyer; *Writer:* Jack Moran; *Key Cast:* Tura Satana (Varla), Haji (Rosie), Lori Williams (Billie); *Cinematography:* Walter Schenk; *Music:* Paul Sawtell and Bert Shefter; *Studio/Distributor:* Eve Productions; *Running Time:* 83 minutes; *Release Date:* 6 August, 1965, USA; *Rating:* NA; *DVD:* NA.

Premise: Three go-go dancers go on a crime spree

Prone to a most feminine hysteria when it came to constructing his plots, Russ Meyer was also notable for the cartoony giantesses with which he populated the screen. In this film, which veers only slightly off the road to film soleil, Meyer and his collaborators fashion a tale that reverses the usual hostage-taking scenario: three vicious go-go dancers on a weekend jaunt to the dunes take a typical American couple hostage and then, later ending up amid a dysfunctional family, seeking to rob their hosts. Meyer's comic view of things makes this excessive. As he did in many areas, Meyer here serves as a barometer of film soleil's later fixation on the evil woman.

1966

The Chase; *Director*: Arthur Penn; *Writer*: Lillian Hellman, from a novel by Horton Foote; *Key Cast*: Marlon Brando (Sheriff Calder), Jane Fonda (Anna Reeves), Robert Redford (Charlie 'Bubber' Reeves), E.G. Marshall (Val Rogers), Angie Dickinson (Ruby Calder); *Cinematography*: Joseph La Shelle and Robert Surtees; *Music*: John Barry; *Studio/Distributor*: Columbia; *Running Time*: 133 minutes; *Release Date*: 19 February, 1966, USA; *Rating*: NR; *DVD*: *Region 1*: Columbia, February 2004, 2.35:1; *Region 2*: NA.

Premise: An escapee finds himself dragged inevitably back to his home town

Chaotic, obvious, blunt, violent, sprawling, Arthur Penn's Southern drama from a screenplay by Lillian Hellman itself, adapted from a play by Horton Foote, is a terrific film. Reviewers at the time lambasted it, and so did later DVD reviewers, often getting their facts wrong. The fact that Penn disowned *The Chase* didn't help. The film was seized by the studio and edited strictly to the script, with the editors usually using the first takes, which were more literal, rather than later takes, where Penn says actors such as Brando and Fonda shone. And it is not as if Penn betrayed a great source. Hellman's screenplay is a complete revision of the play, which is talky, boring, and static, and in which most of the relationships are different. One of the probable reasons why critics and *auteur*-oriented reviewers don't like *The Chase* may be because as a social protest film it is all on the surface. There appears to be no thematic or visual directorial input that, say, a director like Douglas Sirk, would insert. It is what it is. The definitive essay on *The Chase* so far is found in Robin Wood's book *Arthur Penn* (Praeger Film Library, 1970), and he is one of the few critics to regard the film highly, pointing out that the triangle that arises among Redford, Fonda, and Fox is potentially progressive, although the backward social mores that make the town so etiolated also destroy the trio before their progressive notions can even take root. The film is a tragedy of injustice, not just of the legal system, but also of the potential for change.

1967

✳ *Point Blank*; *Director*: John Boorman; *Writer*: Alexander Jacobs, David Newhouse and Rafe Newhouse, from a novel by Richard Stark (Donald E. Westlake); *Key Cast*: Lee Marvin (Walker), Angie Dickinson (Chris), Keenan Wynn (Yost), Carroll O'Connor (Brewster), John Vernon (Mal Reese); *Cinematography*: Philip H. Lathrop; *Music*: Johnny Mandel; *Studio/Distributor*: MGM; *Running Time*: 92 minutes; *Release Date*: 30 August, 1967, USA; *Rating*: NR; *DVD*: *Region 1*: Warner, June 2005, 2.35:1, with director commentary, vintage making ofs; *Region 2*: NA.

Premise: A gangster goes after the betraying friends and mobsters who have his money

A film that gains in prestige with each passing year, *Point Blank* is perfect film soleil, and a movie that was both ahead of its time and also very much of its time. It's just that contemporaries couldn't really see it. Director Boorman drew upon the editing and narrative stylings of the French New Wave to tell what is otherwise a conventional crime story, drawing upon Resnais and Godard especially. But the oneiric quality of the film is in fact very much in keeping with the surrealism of traditional noir. Besides the influence of European films – its jagged editing, temporal displacements, dream like qualities, sexual frankness, and its unpredictable morality – it still has roots in traditional noir, especially in the theme of male friendships betrayed, as found in Wellman and Walsh. It's also oneiric, like a good 1940s noir. But at heart, it is the bedrock persona of Lee Marvin, thumping through the film with grim determination in what some see as a reprise of his character in *The Killers* (Boorman even changed the Stark novels' character's name from Parker to Walker to accommodate his style). Ultimately it doesn't matter if he is a ghost, as some critics maintain, but it is interesting how Boorman and Marvin alternate Walker's great physical presence with the ethereality of a specter (now you see him now you don't). At the time, the film was viewed as taking violence to the extreme; today we see how its pace is in fact rather lugubrious, as if Walker is walking through a dream. *Point Blank* was later remade as *Xia dao Gao Fei* (Ringo Lam, 1993) with Chow Yun Fat and heavily influenced *Payback* (Brian Helgeland, 1999). Other Richard Stark-Parker adaptations include Godard's *Made in USA* (1966), *Pillaged* (Alain Cavalier, 1967), *The Split*, (Gordon Flemyng, 1968) *The Outfit* (John Flynn, 1973), and *Slayground* (Terry Bedford, 1983), suggesting that, like Thompson and James Ellroy, he forms a triumvirate of soleil writers. A whole book could be written on *Point Blank* and I hope someday there is one. It's a great film and the 2005 DVD release fills an aching gap.

1968

Targets; *Director:* Peter Bogdanovich; *Writer:* Bogdan-
ovich and Polly Platt, with Samuel Fuller; *Key Cast:* Tim
O'Kelly (Bobby Thompson), Boris Karloff (Byron Orlok);
Cinematography: Laszlo Kovacs; *Music:* Ronald Stein (from
The Terror); *Studio/Distributor:* Paramount. *Running Time:* 90
minutes; *Release Date:* 15 August, 1968, USA; *Rating:* NR;
DVD: Region 1: Paramount, August 2003, 1.85:1, with
director commentary; *Region 2:* NA.

Premise: A spree killer meets his match in an old horror star

Officially a horror film, *Target's* SoCal setting, its tone of
nostalgia in the face of a coarsening society allows it to stray
into film soleil territory. *Targets* tells two parallel stories that
intersect at the end, both commenting on changing fashions
in psychoses. In the first story, a horror actor named Byron
Orlok (Karloff) is under pressure to appear in the new horror
film written and directed by Sammy Michaels
(Bogdanovich, his character named after Sam Fuller). In the
second story a clean cut young man (Tim O'Kelly) has
quietly gone mad, first killing his family, then some strangers
on a highway, and finally the patrons of a drive in, where
Orlok is set to make an appearance. Bogdanovich always
favored the old over the young, especially when he was
young, and here he shows remarkable sympathy with Orlok's
age and dwindling business concerns. The parody of
Hollywood is a loving parody, but Orlok's grim remarks
about the town while passing by a number of used car lots,
also shows Bogdanovich's identification with the world
weary manner. Karloff brings great dignity to the role and it

is surely one of his best and most engaging performances. Based on Charles Whitman, who shot students on a Texas college campus, the sniper is all-American, calling his father "Sir," and praying before dinner. Bogdanovich doesn't try to penetrate his façade. He observes him from the outside, in jaggedly edited sequences that feel very much like a Fuller film. In a sense, Bogdanovich seems give up. He suggests that there is no understanding for this kind of madness, although shots of Thompson on the freeway eating a candy bar suggest a "Twinkie" defence. In his excellent commentary track for the disc, Bogdanovich describes working with Karloff, who always referred to dialogue as either "the lyrics" or "the jokes."

1969

The Italian Job; *Director:* Peter Collinson; *Writer:* Troy Kennedy Martin; *Key Cast:* Michael Caine (Charlie Croker), Noël Coward (Mr. Bridger), Benny Hill (Professor Simon Peach), Raf Vallone (Altabani); *Cinematography:* Douglas Slocombe; *Music:* Quincy Jones; *Studio/Distributor:* Paramount; *Running Time:* 99 minutes; *Release Date:* 2 June, 1969, UK; *Rating:* G; *DVD: Region 1:* Paramount, October 2003, 1.85:1, with scholar commentary, deleted scenes, making ofs; *Region 2:* August 2002, with same as above.

Premise: A gangster plans the theft of $4 million from an Italian bank

A terribly overrated film, was *The Italian Job* really all that popular when it came out? Paramount went ahead and remade it as if it were. But seeing it today, it lacks the charm, wit, or excitement that it is heralded for. It tells of a gold bullion heist, and in this case the guy behind the caper is the recently released from prison Charlie Croker (Caine). Working, it seems, at the behest of the still incarcerated Mr. Bridger (Noel Coward, in a part that resembles a similar character in the earlier *The Criminal*), Croker assembles a team of crooks, including Benny Hill as a computer whiz with a penchant for the opposite sex that puts you in mind of Sam Jaffe's Achilles Heel in *The Asphalt Jungle*. The plan is elaborate, but as per the genre, you don't really know its full dimensions until it unfolds. Although the crew combats both the cops and the Mafia to get the gold, they end up hanging by a thread in a cliffhanger ending that aspires to the existential absurdity of the *Wages of Fear*. The 2003 remake is solely an action car-chase film.

Additional, Potential, or Honorary Films Soleils: 1960: *The Criminal* [*The Concrete Jungle*]; 1962: *Experiment in Terror*; 1963: *Kanto Wanderer*; 1966: *Harper*; 1967: *The Detective*; 1968: *Blackmail is My Life*.

Early Film Soleil: The 1970s

Hollywood roiled with changes in the 1970s. These changes – the collapse of the studio system, the rise of the movie brats, changes in movie-going habits, the relaxing of the Production Code, competition from foreign films – have been well chronicled. Also pertinent is the rise of such genres as the blaxploitation film and, although nobody knew it at the time, film soleil, both mostly independently financed types of productions. While cop films such as *Dirty Harry* wrestled with the limitations of crime fighting, blaxploitation films, and to a certain extent soleil, reveled in the barely coded evil doings of their protagonists.

1970

Le Bucher; *Director*: Claude Chabrol; *Writer*: Chabrol; *Key Cast*: Stéphane Audran (Helene), Jean Yanne (Popaul); *Cinematography*: Jean Rabier; *Music*: Pierre Jansen; *Studio/Distributor*: EIA (France); *Running Time*: 93 minutes; *Release Date*: 12 September 1970 (New York Film Festival); *Rating*: GP; *DVD*: *Region 1*: Pathfinder, May 2003, 1.85:1, with critic commentary, stills; *Region 2*: NA.

Premise: A spinsterish schoolteacher starts a romance with the local butcher as a serial killer terrorises their village

A profound neutrality descends over Claude Chabrol's film about a serial killer. He doesn't appear to judge the killer, nor does he try to "explain" him. He just *is*. In that light, Chabrol's Popaul anticipates the cinematic serial killer mania of the 1980s (an outgrowth of the teen slasher films of the 1970s). Chabrol, a Hitchcockian in so many subtle as well as obvious ways, does the Hitchcockian thing of placing his killer in the bucolic setting of a middle class French village. He also twists the knife by having Popaul begin to form a relationship with the local schoolteacher, appropriately repressed. Sunlight permeates this nightmarish story, which makes no concessions to the viewer. Robin Buss' *French Film Noir* contains an excellent and detailed discussion of this film.

1971

Road to Salina; *Director*: George Lautner; *Writer*: Lautner, with Pascal Jardin and Jack Miller, from the novel by Maurice Cury; *Key Cast*: Mimsy Farmer (Billie), Robert Walker Jr. (Jonas), Rita Hayworth (Mara), Ed Begley (Warren); *Cinematography*: Maurice Fellous; *Music*: Clinic; *Studio/Distributor*: AVCO Embassy Pictures; *Running Time*: 96 minutes; *Release Date*: 17 February 1971, USA; *Rating*: R; *DVD*: NA.

Premise: A drifter disrupts an already dysfunctional family

Beginning like any typical soleil, with a drifter coming between the isolated residents of some commercial outpost, Lautner's film very quickly becomes something other, a bizarre mélange of incest, drugs, sex, and hallucination. A very minor influence on Tarantino's *Kill Bill*, *Salina* follows many typical noir conventions. It is told in flashback, it involves a murder, and emotions such as greed and jealousy are heightened. But it is all set in a near-lunar desert landscape like something out of Antonioni, and has the added cachet of youth, pitting the very young and hippie-like against the old and decrepit. It's not a very good film, but that makes it more interesting.

1972

✳ **Pulp**; *Director*: Mike Hodges; *Writer*: Hodges; *Key Cast*: Michael Caine (Mickey King), Mickey Rooney (Preston Gilbert), Lionel Stander (Ben Dinuccio), Lizabeth Scott (Princess Betty Cippola), Nadia Cassini (Liz Adams);

Cinematography: Ousama Rawi; *Music*: George Martin; *Studio/Distributor:* UA; *Running Time*: 95 minutes; *Release Date*: 1972, USA; *Rating*: PG; *DVD*: *Region 1*: NA; *Region 2*: MGM, 2004.

Premise: Mobsters are worried that one of their own may unveil secrets in his forthcoming memoir

An exercise in nostalgia, *Pulp*, like *Road to Salina*, blends old timers and youngsters in a sunny continental setting. It also has a comical, if not lax, take on the criminal industry, while embedding a very serious critique of the abuse of power beneath the frivolity. Its plot is too complex but also too much fun to summarise here. Suffice it to say that Mike Hodges' follow up to *Get Carter* is a gem well worth revisiting or catching up with.

✳ ***Beverly Hills Nightmare*** [*Bone; The Housewife*]; *Director:* Larry Cohen; *Writer:* Cohen; *Key Cast:*Yaphet Kotto (Bone), Andrew Duggan (Bill), Joyce Van Patten (Bernadette); *Cinematography*: George Folsey, Jr.; *Music*: Gil Melle; *Studio/Distributor:* James H. Harris. *Running Time*: 95 minutes; *Release Date*: July, 1972, USA; *Rating*: R; *DVD*: *Region 1*: Blue Underground, August 2003, 1.85:1, with director commentary, producer interview, alternate scenes, poster and still gallery; *Region 2*: NA.

Premise: A thief becomes in involved in the life of a Beverly Hills couple

A blend of *Who's Afraid of Virginia Woolf* and *Teorema*, Larry Cohen's film inserts a "scary" African-American intruder into a corrupted rich white family, where he then proceeds to unravel its already fragile stability. The film is jerky, nervous, agitated, with fantasy and "reality" alternating in an uneasy alliance. Indeed, at the film's end it is unclear if Bone really existed, or if the corruption of white society even *needed* him there to help destroy itself. As Bone and his female victim gradually unite in a *Postman*-style plan to eliminate her husband, Bone himself gradually begins to adopt some of the bourgeois values and complaints that the husband expressed at the film's start. Cohen also includes an interesting sub-theme about the hazards of movies, media, and even movie theaters as social gathering places.

✳ *Prime Cut*; *Director*: Michael Ritchie; *Writer*: Robert Dillon; *Key Cast*: Lee Marvin (Nick Devlin), Gene Hackman (Mary Ann), Sissy Spacek (Poppy), Eddie Egan (Jake); *Cinematography*: Gene Polito; *Music*: Lalo Schifrin; *Studio/Distributor*: Cinema Center Films/National General; *Running Time*: 88 minutes; *Release Date*: 28 June, 1972, USA; *Rating*: R; *DVD*: *Region 1*: Paramount, June 2005, 2.35:1; *Region 2*: NA.

Premise: A Chicago enforcer is sent on an errand to Kansas

Prime Cut is an interesting if not wholly successful film. Like some of the British crime films of the 1960s, it is set completely in the amoral world of criminals, who have varyingly strict private codes of behavior. Lee Marvin, once again an enforcer, is sent from Chicago to Kansas to push back into line a renegade (Gene Hackman) where many before have failed (*The French Connection*'s real-life cop Eddie Egan has a cameo as the head of Chicago's Irish mob). Enacting a code of justice within injustice, Marvin rescues some young conscripted hookers while taking down Hackman's enterprise. Michael Ritchie's film was reputedly re-cut or changed on him, and the resultant film lacks zest in its action scenes, but as an offbeat example of film soleil it is fascinating.

❋ *The Mechanic*; *Director*: Michael Winner; *Writer*: Lewis John Carlino; *Key Cast*: Charles Bronson (Arthur Bishop), Jan-Michael Vincent (Steve McKenna), Keenan Wynn (Harry McKenna); *Cinematography*: Richard H. Kline and Robert Paynter; *Music*: Jerry Fielding; *Studio/Distributor*: UA; *Running Time*: 100 minutes; *Release Date*: 17 November, 1972, USA; *Rating*: PG; *DVD*: *Region 1*: MGM, October 2002, 1.85:1 and full frame; *Region 2*: NA.

Premise: A paid assassin takes on a young apprentice

There's a great cult film inside *The Mechanic* but it needed a great director to get it out. Unfortunately, it got Michael Winner. Usually he is a mundane movie helmer with no distinguishing visual characteristics except a penchant for kinky sex. Action star Charles Bronson had formed some kind of Satanic pact with the British Winner in the 1970s and *The Mechanic,* their second film, remains one of the more interesting of their collaborations. After this, they did *Death Wish,* and everything went to hell. Bronson is Arthur Bishop, hit man for a vague *Point Blank*-style "commission" of anonymous gangsters. He's one of those sophisticated killers ("Murder is only killing without a license") who works alone and works slowly, studying pix of his victim and the victim's environment as he drinks brandy from a snifter and listens to classical music. Bishop has a few problems, however. He's wound a little tight, and, like Tony Soprano, is subject to anxiety-related fainting spells. They are due to his relationship with his father, who was a rather cold gangster who once allowed his son to almost drown while teaching him to swim. The only form of intimacy he has is a relationship with a hooker (Bronson's wife Jill Ireland) whom he pays to act like she loves him. Into this isolation comes Steve McKenna (Jan-Michael Vincent), the son of an old colleague (Keenan Wynn) of Bishop's father. Bishop reluctantly takes on the irresponsible, cold-hearted, and selfish kid as an apprentice and they do a couple of hits together until it seems as if Bishop's bosses are set to turn on him. The movie is written by playwright-turned-screenwriter Lewis John Carlino, who is something of an ur-John Milius or James Toback. Carlino composed some nice scenes for *The Mechanic*. The film opens with a great sequence chronicling one of Bishop's hits, which includes some great window snooping voyeurism in the tradition of *Rear Window*. The film ends with an exciting chase down the Italian coast that anticipates a similar chase scene in the later *Ronin*. What Winner brings to the package is a tilt to the ludicrous. What is all Carlino is the barely disguised homoerotic subtext. The first sight of Vincent is of his buttocks, and there is an attraction-competition between the older man and his young, raw recruit. The 1972 Signet novelisation, also written by Carlino, makes the homoeroticism more explicit. One of the pair even places a full-mouthed kiss on the lips of the other as he dies. The film is a character study more than a story, and Bronson is adept at capturing the pained creature beneath the scary brute. The camera lovingly dwells on his ugly beauty. It's not everyone who can carry a film like this, a blend of action and morbid psychology. One laments that Bronson didn't have better career choices in directors and projects. Footnote: the US DVD comes with the addition of a scratchy full frame trailer with a different re-release title (*Killer of Killers*) narrated by someone who apparently hasn't seen the film "One man who does what the police won't do. What the government can't do. He stops the underworld dead in its tracks." There is no mention that Bronson's character *is* the underworld.

❋ *The Getaway*; *Director:* Sam Peckinpah; *Writer:* Walter Hill, from a novel by Jim Thompson; *Key Cast:* Steve McQueen (Carter 'Doc' McCoy), Ali MacGraw (Carol Ainsley McCoy), Ben Johnson (Jack Beynon), Sally Struthers (Fran Clinton), Al Lettieri (Rudy Butler); *Cinematography:* Lucian Ballard; *Music:* Quincy Jones; *Studio/Distributor:* Warner; *Running Time:* 122 minutes; *Release Date:* 13 December, 1972, USA; *Rating:* PG; *DVD:* *Region 1:* Warner, May 2005, 2.40:1, with audio commentary by four Peckinpah scholars, and special featurette; *Region 2:* November 1998.

Premise: A woman arranges to have her husband sprung from jail

Based on a Thompson novel (though changing the apocalyptic ending), Peckinpah's version of *The Getaway* continues the director's love affair with the West, with rogues, with romance as a title fight, and with Mexico as the go-to place when things get hot. Peckinpah's intercut slo-mo scenes can often seem arbitrary and no more so than here, but the real weight of the film rests on McQueen and MacGraw's on screen relationship (fueled by one off screen). It's as if Peckinpah were offering up his ideal of marriage (though it should be noted that the film was greatly influenced by McQueen, as producer and in other silent capacities). In contrast is Lettieri's bullying bank robber, who takes a weakling and his wife hostage and proves catnip to the woman. In its twisted, nightmarish way, and in its harsh amoral world, McQueen's bank robber and his moll prove to be the moral center.

1973

The Long Goodbye; *Director*: Robert Altman; *Writer*: Leigh Brackett, from a novel by Raymond Chandler; *Key Cast*: Elliott Gould (Philip Marlowe), Nina van Pallandt (Eileen Wade), Sterling Hayden (Roger Wade), Mark Rydell (Marty Augustine), Henry Gibson (Dr. Verringer), Jim Bouton (Terry Lennox); *Cinematography*: Vilmos Zsigmond; *Music*: John Williams; *Studio/Distributor*: UA; *Running Time*: 112 minutes; *Release Date*: 7 March, 1973, USA; *Rating*: R; *DVD*: *Region 1*: MGM, September 2002, 2.35:1, with making of, cinematography featurette, *American Cinematographer* article, radio ads; *Region 2*: NA.

Premise: A private eye disrupts the family that hired him

"He turned and walked across the floor and out. I watched the door close. I listened to his steps going away down the imitation marble corridor. After a while they got faint, then they got silent. I kept on listening anyway. What for? Did I want him to stop suddenly and turn and come back and talk me out of the way I felt? Well, he didn't. That was the last I saw of him. I never saw any of them again – except the cops. No way has yet been invented to say goodbye to them."

That's how Raymond Chandler ends his last magnificent Philip Marlowe novel, *The Long Goodbye*. It's a moment of defeat. Marlowe has been confronted by the manipulative genius behind the mystery that he has been pursuing through this, Chandler's longest novel. Terry Lennox, who up until this moment has been presumed dead, confronts Marlowe quietly in his office. Marlowe was a friend of Terry's, and you could say that Marlowe was a little bit in love with him, the way working stiffs often fall in love with handsome rich guys with charismatic if dissipating ways. Lennox is confronting Marlowe and it is the final act of betrayal. Lennox used Marlowe. He played him for a sap. But the last vestige of sympathy in Lennox's soul compels him to make a final visit to Marlowe in his office to try to explain himself. Marlowe won't have any of it. The code by which Marlowe is judging Lennox is unstated, but it fills the entire big novel that precedes this scene. It's powerful and sad, in the way that only really good detective novels about men who must tell the truth and express their hidden emotions through sarcasm can be. That's not the way that Robert Altman's 1973 adaptation of the book ends. In the film, Marlowe drives down to Mexico and shoots Lennox, busting up the rogue's dreams of escape. If Marlowe's action in the movie seems something of an overreaction, that's because the sense of betrayal is never really very clear in either book or movie, and Marlowe's *beau geste* is the act of a futile, confused, and out of joint man. Altman was on quite a roll by the time he got to *The Long Goodbye*, making "anti" movies. *M*A*S*H* (1970) was an anti-war film, *McCabe and Mrs. Miller* an anti-western, *Images* an anti-thriller. He followed *The Long Goodbye* with *Thieves Like Us,* a mock road film, and *California Split,* a mock gambling film. But having spewed out his contempt for cinema and its genres in the early 1970s, he seems to have nothing left to say or hate. There is no doubt that Altman is an auteur in the conventional sense. His films are all of a piece, with their floating cameras, zooms, stock company, and multiple audio tracks. But Altman is so motivated by rage and anger and disappointment that he has soured on everything. So when he confronts the masculine romanticism of Chandler's novel, he has to mock and betray it, the way Lennox betrays Marlowe. Altman seemed personally offended by Marlowe. On the set he passed around copies of the then-hard-to-find Chandler letter and essay collection *Raymond Chandler Speaking,* eager for his cast and crew to note the suicidal tendencies behind Chandler's romanticism. He worked from a screenplay by Hawks collaborator and sci-fi writer Leigh Brackett, who wrote *The Big Sleep,* to assure that the film would have some linkages back to Hollywood detective films, just so he could undermine them. And he updated the story from the early 1950s to the 1970s, with Marlowe out of touch, a man in a blue 1940s suit and an old car, a guy with a cat instead of a girlfriend, and a buffoon who is the tool of those around him. The worst thing Altman does is take away Marlowe's voice. It is not a "first person movie," it is a Robert Altman movie, with quirky casting (*Laugh-In's* Henry Gibson, Hughes forgery squeeze Nina Van Pallandt, ex-baseball star Jim Bouton as Lennox) and a style that diffuses everyone. The movie of *The Long Goodbye* is an outrageous betrayal but with a few good parts. The slow zoom showing Hemingwayesque writer Sterling Hayden walking into the sea to commit suicide while Marlowe and the man's wife argue about him is justly famous, but again it's turning a first person caper into a first person director log; and there was the clever idea of the multiple iterations of the movie's theme song, written by John Williams and Johnny Mercer, heard as everything from grocery store Muzak to doorbell chimes. Parts of the film, then, are fine. But for the most part the film is a travesty. Yet here it is. It exists, and it won't go away. One can only hope that, once enough time has passed and the mood of the world changes, someone with the same sort of dedication as the people who made *L. A. Confidential* will try it again.

✻ *Badlands*; *Director*: Terrence Malick; *Writer*: Malick; *Key Cast*: Martin Sheen (Kit Carruthers), Sissy Spacek (Holly Sargis), Warren Oates (Holly's father); *Cinematography*: Tak Fujimoto; *Music*: Gunild Keetman, James Taylor, and George Tipton; *Studio/Distributor*: Warner; *Running Time*: 95 minutes; *Release Date*: 15 October, 1973, USA; *Rating*: PG; *DVD*: *Region 1*: Warner, April 1999, 1.85:1, remastered in DD 5.1; *Region 2*: NA.

Premise: A drifter and a teen girl go on a killing spree

Coming at a pivotal time in the history of movies, when the studio system was beginning to break down yet young movie-bred filmmakers were making some of the best films ever, *Badlands* is absolutely not the kind of movie that previous generations of cinema-goers were used to. It views its amoral characters dispassionately. It renders horrific acts in beautiful images. It buys into youth culture. In essence it retells the story of teens Charles Starkweather and Carol Fugate, who killed some 10 people on a spree in Nebraska in 1958. Relocating the action to South Dakota and condensing the time span, Malick takes the comical, brutish inarticulateness of his characters seriously and attempts to tell the story almost wholly visually. Sheen's Kit is insane. Rescuing a household appliance from the wreckage of his girlfriend's house is more important to him than the murder of her father. Malick here attempts something that one realises later should probably be obvious in moviemaking, i.e., telling the story visually, through framing, colour, movement, staging. Yet most movies continue to be literary, telling stories through dialogue. Malick's achievement gains in importance with the years.

1974

The Parallax View; *Director*: Alan J. Pakula; *Writer:* Lorenzo Semple, Jr., David Giler, Robert Towne, from the novel by Loren Singer; *Key Cast*: Warren Beatty (Joseph Frady), Hume Cronyn (Bill Rintels), William Daniels (Austin Tucker); *Cinematography*: Gordon Willis; *Music*: Michael Small; *Studio/Distributor:* Paramount; *Running Time*: 102 minutes; *Release Date*: 14 June, 1974, USA; *Rating*: R; *DVD*: Region 1: Paramount, June 1999, 2.35:1; *Region 2*: NA.

Premise: A small town journalist stumbles onto a vast assassination conspiracy

An example of paranoia noir, along with *The Conversation* (Coppola, 1974), *Winter Kills* (Richert, 1979), and *All the President's Men* (Pakula, 1976), *The Parallax View* is the most radical view of society of at least these titles. It posits a secret government, agency or corporation that impersonally assassinates key political figures, leaving an Oswald-like patsy in their wake to take the blame. Beatty's fumbling Northwest America reporter is too small a figure to take on such a monolithic entity and Pakula's film quietly observes his destruction at the hands of anonymous, powerful figures. It's beautifully done. Pakula had the help of a great visualiser in most of his films (Gordon Willis), and was a superb director of actors, most of whom gave their most realistic performances for him.

❋ *Chinatown*; *Director*: Roman Polanski; *Writer*: Robert Towne; *Key Cast*: Jack Nicholson (Jake Gittes), Faye Dunaway (Evelyn Mulwray), John Huston (Noah Cross); *Cinematography*: John Alonzo; *Music*: Jerry Goldsmith; *Studio/Distributor*: Paramount; *Running Time*: 131 minutes; *Release Date*: 20 June, 1974, USA; *Rating*: R; *DVD*: *Region 1*: Paramount, November 1999, 2.35:1, interview with film-makers; *Region 2*: Paramount, October, 2000.

Premise: A cynical PI finds himself in over his head

"The middle of a drought and the water commissioner dies. Only in LA" Thus speaks the resident medical examiner and thus are summarised *Chinatown*'s numerous paradoxes. *Chinatown* is a key entry in the history of film soleil and an important transitional film, drawing on traditional film noir while showing the way to its successor genre. Although set in the 1930s, opening with illustrated titles and lush music, and using such noir elements as the (seemingly) femme fatale and a private eye on a case, the film is set mostly in day light, indeed in the middle of a heat wave, and it ends on a decidedly dark note, in a sequence the key filmmakers fought over, in which evil triumphs utterly. Although writer Towne and director Polanski draw on common noir tropes, as they tell of a private detective used as a tool in a conspiracy among the elites of Los Angeles to take control of the city's water, the film's true subject is history and politics, not the boyish he-man fantasies of moviegoers. Nixon resigned some six weeks after the release of *Chinatown*, and the film seems to be a product of a darkening of the American political spirit, so perhaps its true heirs are the films of political paranoia noir mentioned above, such as *The Parallax View*, and others. Polanski, in Andrew Sarris' term, "tilted" *Chinatown* toward tragedy, but like *Peeper* (Hyams, 1975) – although comically – *Night Moves*, and *The Long Goodbye* it also undermined common notions of detective heroism and ingenuity, perhaps most famously in the sequence in which detective Jake Gittes learns of a character's parentage. Gittes is more like an anti-hero of later soleils, selfish, greedy, and at times obtuse, but the viewer is invited to later piece together the reasons for what is in fact a newfound cynicism. There is also something achingly beautiful and poignant in the fact that the most moral man in the movie is the one we never really meet, water commissioner Hollis Mulwray (Darrell Zwerling).

Mr. Majestyk; *Director:* Richard Fleischer; *Writer:* Elmore Leonard; *Key Cast:* Charles Bronson (Vince Majestyk), Al Lettieri (Frank Renda), Lee Purcell (Wiley), Paul Koslo (Bobby Kopas); *Cinematography:* Richard H. Kline; *Music:* Charles Bernstein; *Studio/Distributor:* UA; *Running Time:* 103 minutes; *Release Date:* 17 July, 1974, USA; *Rating:* PG; *DVD:* Region 1: MGM, Feb 2003, 1.85:1 and full frame, trailer; Region 2: NA.

Premise: A rancher bucks up against the mob and a mafia chieftain on the run

Mr. Majestyk is one of the few really interesting Bronson programmers, probably because of the accident of having a competent director (Richard Fleischer) on board, and because it was written by Elmore Leonard. It's a typical Leonard story insofar as a kidnapping plays a significant role in the plot (one of Leonard's identifying signatures). In this case it is a gangster named Frank Renda (Lettieri), a hit man for the mob who has somehow managed to get himself arrested. In a prison break out, Renda ends up the prisoner of fellow inmate Vince Majestyk. He's a Colourado melon farmer who is being victimised by a local hood named Kopas (Paul Koslo, a familiar character actor of the time). The point of all this torturous exposition is to get Renda mad at Majestyk so that the whole thing can build to a face-off between the experienced killer and the land and liberty-defending farmer. Although for some reason everyone is pretending that California is really Colourado, and the love interest is perfunctory, *Mr. Majestyk* has much to recommend it. The breakout sequence is well done, with action staged clearly and understandably, unlike so many of today's actioners. A "melon assassination" scene is memorable. Bronson is interesting as a guy who goes up against both the law and the mob, but with a jokey insouciance that you don't usually associate with the star. And good character actors pop up throughout the film, including Lee Purcell as Renda's squeeze. Lettieri, who died in 1975, is absolutely brilliant as the gangster.

1975

❋ ***Night Moves***; *Director:* Arthur Penn; *Writer:* Alan Sharp; *Key Cast:* Gene Hackman (Harry Moseby), Jennifer Warren (Paula), Susan Clark (Ellen Moseby); *Cinematography:* Bruce

Surtees; *Music*: Michael Small; *Studio/Distributor*: Warner; *Running Time*: 100 minutes; *Release Date*: 11 June 1975, USA; *Rating*: R; *DVD*: NA.

Premise: A detective finds himself embroiled in a confusing case

Arthur Penn, in collaboration with Warren Beatty on *Bonnie and Clyde* (1967), could be said to have started it all, if by "it" one means heightened cinematic violence, amoral heroines whom the viewer is invited to admire or empathise with, and European-inflected visual techniques. Beatty was in fact one of the first "inmates" to take over the closed, stolid Hollywood asylum. *Bonnie And Clyde* redefined movies, and in a sense *Night Moves* is the result. Like Altman's *The Long Goodbye*, it is an anti-mystery, although more "existential," positing that no mystery can be truly solved, that human activity is futile, and that heroes are false. In his antipathy to art, Hackman's Moseby is like Meeker's Hammer. But his blundering may lay waste to the things around him, as does Hammer's, but nothing is "solved." This disdainful, hyper-intellectual approach is as unsatisfying as *The Long Goodbye*'s undermining of the genre, at least on a level of popular, satisfying commercial plot mechanics, but it's somehow more acceptable because the viewer senses that Penn and his writers are struggling with changes in the art form and in society at large.

1976

✸: *Assault on Precinct 13*; *Director*: John Carpenter; *Writer*: Carpenter; *Key Cast*: Austin Stoker (Ethan Bishop), Darwin

Joston (Napoleon Wilson), Laurie Zimmer (Leigh), Nancy Kyes [billed as Loomis] (Julie); *Cinematography*: Douglas Knapp; *Music*: Carpenter; *Studio/Distributor*: CKK; *Running Time*: 91 minutes; *Release Date*: 5 November, 1976, USA; *Rating*: R; *DVD*: *Region 1*: numerous DVDs, but the most recent is Image, November, 2004, 2.35:1, with director commentary, video interviews, stills, storyboards, radio ads; *Region 2*: NA.

Premise: LA gang members surround a soon-to-be decommissioned police station

Imagine *Night of the Living Dead* married to *Rio Bravo*, and you've got it: non-stop hoards of multi-ethnic hoods who don't care if they live or die laying siege to a soon-to-be abandoned police station in retaliation for a cop crackdown on gangs. There are many things to love about this movie: the stoicism of the late Darwin Joston as Napoleon Wilson (a character who was a forerunner of Carpenter's Eastmanesque Snake Plissken); the way Tony Burton, as the character Wells, says, "I'm doomed" (and he's right); the outrageousness and guts of killing a little girl on screen. Oh, and of course Laurie Zimmer as Leigh. With her, Carpenter created the near-perfect screen heroine, a modern Angie Dickinson, the epitome of Carpenter's obsession with Hemingway-Hawksian performance skills. Like some of the other "movie brats" versed in the works of Hawks, Hitchcock, and Ford, such as Peter Bogdanovich, Carpenter has a lack of interest in the present, and pines for a past he didn't experience and perhaps only even existed in movies. "There are no heroes anymore, Bishop. Just men who follow orders," says one of the characters, and this Peckinpahesque lament over

84

changing times serves as the Saturday afternoon movie level spine that runs through the conflicts in most of Carpenter's subsequent movies.

1977

✳ *Sorcerer*; *Director:* William Friedkin; *Writer:* Walon Green, from the novel by Georges Arnaud; *Key Cast:* Roy Scheider (Jackie Scanlon), Bruno Cremer (Victor Manzon), Francisco Rabal (Nilo), Amidou (Kassem); *Cinematography*: Dick Bush and John M. Stephens; *Music*: Tangerine Dream; *Studio/Distributor:* Paramount; *Running Time*: 121 minutes; *Release Date*: 24 June, 1977, USA; *Rating*: PG; *DVD*: *Region 1*: Paramount, November 1998, 1.33:1, with web links; *Region 2*: NA.

Premise: Same as *The Wages of Fear*

Though critically reviled (how *dare* Friedkin remake *The Wages of Fear!*) upon its initial release (except for the lone voice of Jack Kroll in *Newsweek*), *Sorcerer* is in fact superior to both its model and the novel from which both are loosely taken. One of the innovations that Friedkin and credited screenwriter Walon Green (*The Wild Bunch*) included is to introduce the four protagonists via opening vignettes. Thus the viewer can care (or not care) about their plight. Friedkin is the poet of frustration, also fully realised in *The French Connection*, but here despair and futility have an unusual physical manifestation as the men tug, plow, drive, bang, and hack their way through their environment. One of the film's numerous thematic threads seems to be that coping with frustration is the "journey" of life. Therefore, the cliffhanger

ending (excellently set up, with at least three vengeful or
mercenary forces waiting to pounce on Roy Scheider's
Jackie Scanlon) is not as despairing as Clouzot's original is
interpreted to be. Scanlon has gotten out of jams just as tight.
Tangerine Dream's driving, yet oft-times also poignant,
music is beautifully matched to the relentless surge of the
two nitro-burdened trucks but also to the beauty of the
landscape and the tones of the men's various emotional
states.

1978

✸ *The Driver*; *Director*: Walter Hill; *Writer:* Hill; *Key Cast*:
Ryan O'Neal (The Driver), Bruce Dern (The Detective),
Isabelle Adjani (The Player), Ronee Blakley (The
Connection), Matt Clark (Plainclothesman); *Cinematography*:
Philip Lathrop; *Music*: Michael Small; *Studio/Distributor:* Fox;
Running Time: 91 minutes; *Release Date*: 28 July, 1978, USA;
Rating: R; *DVD*: *Region 1*: Fox, June 2005, 1.78:1, with alter-
nate opening; *Region 2*: Kinowelt, July 2001.

Premise: Cops track an elusive heist getaway man

It's a little bit of a cheat to categorise *The Driver* as a film
soleil. For one thing, it was famously filmed mostly at night,
on the wide streets of downtown Los Angeles over the
course of several weeks. But although its creatures are
nocturnal, the film qualifies as a modified soleil thanks to its
hagiographic portrayal of a man, the unnamed getaway
driver played by O'Neal, living outside the law but within
his own code. In fact he lives a code so severe it excludes
almost everyone else, as per the film's general model, Jean-

Pierre Melville's *Le Samourai* (1967). As an effort to transplant the spirit and existential angst of European films to Hollywood, *The Driver* falls in with *Bonnie and Clyde*, *Point Blank*, and the later remake of *A Bout de Soufflé*, *Breathless*. On the one hand, director Hill strives to rework a sequence he must have felt that Sam Peckinpah messed up in an earlier incarnation in the script of *The Getaway* (a distracting sequence on a train); on the other, the film leads with its strength (an elaborate car chase that, by today's standards, beggars believability) and then has little where else to go. Also, Hill renders the driver so opaque that the viewer can't really relate to him, unlike Melville's Samurai, who has a streak of sentimentality, even though it is presented as a tragic flaw leading to his demise.

✹ *Who'll Stop the Rain*; *Director:* Karel Reisz; *Writer:* Judith Rascoe and Robert Stone, from the novel *Dog Soldiers* by Stone; *Key Cast:* Nick Nolte (Ray Hicks), Tuesday Weld (Marge Converse), Michael Moriarty (John Converse), Anthony Zerbe (Antheil), Ray Sharkey (Smitty); *Cinematography:* Richard H. Kline; *Music:* Laurence Rosenthal; *Studio/Distributor:* UA; *Running Time:* 126 minutes; *Release Date:* 2 August, 1978, USA; *Rating:* R; *DVD: Region 1*: MGM, July 2001, 1.85:1, with original trailer; *Region 2*: NA.

Premise: A vet helps a writer smuggle heroin

Visually undistinguished, edited competently, and with a story that makes nod to contemporary issues (Vietnam, drugs), *Who'll Stop the Rain* (or how we would prefer to call it by its rightful title, *Dog Soldiers*!) is a movie that is sustained by its excellent casting and acting. In a less somber or realistic movie, Nick Nolte's Ray Hicks would get the girl and get the money, but in the realm of soleil, he gets neither, yet remains the most honorable and competent among the film's characters. "All my life I've been taking shit from inferior people," he complains at one point. "No more." The whole cast is excellent but especially delightful is Anthony Zerbe as the manipulative, contemptuous villain, a role that Robert Ryan would have played if the film were made 20 years earlier.

1979

Hardcore [*The Hardcore Life*]; *Director*: Paul Schrader; *Writer*: Schrader; *Key Cast*: George C. Scott (Jake Van Dorn), Peter Boyle (Andy Mast), Season Hubley (Niki); *Cinematography*: Michael Chapman; *Music*: Jack Nitzsche; *Studio/Distributor*: Columbia; *Running Time*: 109 minutes; *Release Date*: 9 February, 1979, USA; *Rating*: R; *DVD*: *Region 1*: Columbia-Tristar, September 2004, 1.85:1; *Region 2*: NA.

Premise: A middle class father searches for his daughter in the LA porn industry

Season Hubley's Niki is the "Ophelia" of this story of a descent into hell, the real heart of the movie and just as cast aside in the end. She is assisting George C. Scott's Jake in finding his daughter, who has somehow entered the world of dirty movies. As in the later *8mm*, Jake must descend into the labyrinthine world of smut, which gets dirtier and kinkier the lower he sinks to the bottom. In his search for her, the film is something of a darker version of Milos Forman's

Taking Off (1971) and of *Joe* (Avildsen, 1970). But if she is the hooker with the heart of gold in this hardcore world, Jake adds a double meaning to the title: his Calvinism is equally hardcore. Unfortunately, *Hardcore* is more of a great idea for a movie than a fully realised project, and as a "journey" or "quest" film it fits well into current theologies about how screenplays can and should work. Paradoxically, it is not funny enough, and the last few minutes (reunion of father and daughter) seem rushed and "inorganic" to what has gone before. It was Paul Schrader's second film as a director, and is obviously highly personal in some ways since he came out of the same milieu as Jake. Unfortunately, it doesn't *feel* personal. It feels icy and chilly and you grasp quickly that Schrader is at root taking the "side" of Jake regardless of however much sympathy he accords to Niki. It's an "incoherent text," because Schrader wants to judge Sodom, without admitting how much appeal it had and has for him. Still, the texture of the film is enhanced by the harsh, judgmental score of Jack Nitzsche, one of the key composers of this era of film soleil.

Additional, Potential, or Honorary Film Soleil: 1970: *Le Cercle Rouge;* 1971: *The Last Run, Get Carter, Klute, The French Connection, Gumshoe, Dirty Harry;* 1972: *Hickey and Boggs, The Godfather;* 1973: *The Friends of Eddie Coyle, The Outfit, The Laughing Policeman;* 1974: *Bring Me the Head of Alfredo Garcia, The Conversation;* 1975: *Hustle, The Nickel Ride, The French Connection II, The Drowning Pool;* 1976: *The Killer Inside Me, Obsession;* 1977: *Rolling Thunder;* 1978: *Blue Collar, Fingers, Day of the Woman [I Spit on Your Grave].*

The 1980s

If a comprehensive poll were possible, it's likely that as the 1980s would end up as the least liked cinematic decade. As the studios flailed around to redefine themselves, the exciting movie brat dramas of the 1970s were overtaken by the new old-time-serial based movies of Lucas and Spielberg. There was another influx of European directors, to match the 1930s, and connoisseurs of cinema were finding their interest drifting to Hong Kong and Australia. Hollywood's indecision and weariness was eradicated when it discovered the 'siege' movie: *Die Hard* and its many successors, which caused the industry to get bogged down in blockbuster openings. Still, the 1980s has much to recommend it: the beginnings of a revitalisation of the indie feature movement and an often shockingly frank confrontation with politics (in *Missing*, *Under Fire*, *Salvador* and others), both trends feeding into the actual birth of film soleil.

1981

Cutter and Bone; *Director*: Ivan Passer; *Writer:* Jeffrey Alan Fiskin from the novel by Newton Thornburg; *Key Cast*: Jeff Bridges (Richard Bone), John Heard (Alex Cutter), Lisa Eichhorn (Maureen Cutter), Ann Dusenberry (Valerie Duran); *Cinematography*: Jordan Cronenweth; *Music*: Jack Nitzsche; *Studio/Distributor*: UA; *Running Time*: 105 minutes; *Release Date*: 20 March, 1981, USA; *Rating*: R; *DVD*: *Region 1*: MGM, January, 2005, 1.85:1; *Region 2*: NA.

Premise: Two Vietnam vets try to solve a murder

Based on an intense novel by Newton Thornburg, *Cutter and Bone* is a complex tale of anger and lost dreams. It takes a trio of disparate characters – a pretty boy, a damaged Vietnam vet, and his drug addicted wife – and sets them the task of solving a crime for which one of them was initially accused. Heard's Alex takes this opportunity to turn their amateur murder investigation into a referendum against American society and its involvement in Vietnam, but the tragedy of the film and its characters is much larger than a mere political tract. Underrated by most reviewers but a festival favorite, *Cutter and Bone* failed to find an audience, probably because the public was more interested in upbeat, self-congratulatory tales at the time. Cinematographer Jordan Cronenweth is to film soleil what John Alton was to traditional noir.

The Postman Always Rings Twice; *Director*: Bob Rafelson; *Writer*: David Mamet from the James M. Cain novel; *Key Cast*: Jack Nicholson (Frank Chambers), Jessica Lange (Cora Papadakis), John Colicos (Nick Papadakis); *Cinematography*: Sven Nykvist; *Music*: Michael Small; *Studio/Distributor*: Paramount; *Running Time*: 122 minutes; *Release Date*: 20 March, 1981, USA; *Rating*: R; *DVD*: Region 1: August, 1997, pan and scan; Region 2: NA.

Premise: Same as the 1946 version

A terribly unenergetic rehash of the earlier film of Cain's novel with the modern "selling point" of more explicit glimpses of the animal lust that erupts between the diner owner's wife and the drifter. Freedom from the Production Code does not encourage the filmmakers to come up with anything as subversively clever as the rolling lipstick tube in Garnett's film.

✳ *Body Heat*; *Director*: Lawrence Kasdan; *Writer*: Kasdan; *Key Cast*: William Hurt (Ned Racine), Kathleen Turner (Matty Walker), Richard Crenna (Edmund Walker), Ted Danson (Peter Lowenstein); *Cinematography*: Richard H. Kline; *Music*: John Barry; *Studio/Distributor*: Warner; *Running Time*: 113 minutes; *Release Date*: 28 August, 1981, USA; *Rating*: R; *DVD*: *Region 1*: Warner, November 1997, 1.85:1; *Region 2*: Warner, September 1998.

Premise: A mediocre lawyer falls for a married woman

Body Heat is a key, defining film soleil. It is an excellent film in the American 'Tradition of Quality' that the French New Wave critics so decried (yet then came to respect once they became filmmakers themselves). It takes noir elements – the *Postman-Indemnity* premise of a married woman soliciting a lover to help her eliminate a wealthy husband – and rings subtle, witty, and influential changes on it. The femme fatale, for example, is fatale to the nth degree and in the end does *not* prove to be hiding a heart of gold. And the hero is kinda dumb (and in one of the film's many funny lines, Turner's Matty even tells him she likes that in a man). A career-making endeavor for most of its participants, *Body Heat* also has a lasting influence, becoming the sort of 'go-to' noir that subsequent films (such as *Wild Things*) sought to emulate instead of the early, traditional noir more often associated with that kind of complex, twisty plot.

✳ *Coup de Torchon* [*Clean Slate*]; *Director*: Bertrand Tavernier; *Writer*: Tavernier, and Jean Aurenche from the novel by Jim

Thompson; *Key Cast*: Philippe Noiret (Lucien Cordier),
Isabelle Huppert (Rose), Stéphane Audran (Huguette
Cordier); *Cinematography*: Pierre-William Glenn; *Music*:
Philippe Sarde; *Studio/Distributor*: Quartet Films; *Running
Time*: 128 minutes; *Release Date*: 4 November 1981, France;
Rating: NA; *DVD*: Region 1: March 2001, 1.66:1, with video
interview and alternate ending; *Region 2*: NA.

Premise: A small town cop isn't as dumb as he looks

"I thought it was the judgment day," two entirely separate
characters say about sudden weather changes at different
points far distant from each other, the first near the beginning, the second near the end of this film. It's a Jim
Thompson adaptation that changes almost everything from
the source book but the apocalyptic spirit of Thompson
himself. But it is not meteorological shifts that change the
small world of colonial Africa (the film was shot in Senegal).
It is chief cop Lucien Cordier (Noiret) who, finally fed up,
contrives to either kill his numerous foes or have them kill
each other, visiting upon them with great vengeance and
furious anger a form of amateur judgment. Cordier is the
quintessential Thompson hero. He is a lower class individual,
in many ways a lazy vulgarian whom everyone treats with
contempt but whom everyone in fact also underestimates.
Here, *Yojimbo*-like, Cordier essentially sets the various
factions against each other. There are also hints, at least in the
book (some typographical) that he is making everything up.
But the movie is much more interested in providing old time
movie satisfaction by having Cordier best everyone, while
still ending on an ambiguous note. Are his days of judgment
over, or has Cordier found new victims?

1982

The Border; *Director*: Tony Richardson; *Writer*: David Freeman, Walon Green, and Deric Washburn; *Key Cast*: Jack Nicholson (Charlie Smith), Harvey Keitel (Cat), Valerie Perrine (Marcy), Warren Oates (Red); *Cinematography*: Ric Waite; *Music*: Ry Cooder; *Studio/Distributor*: Universal; *Running Time*: 109 minutes; *Release Date*: 31 January, 1982, USA; *Rating*: R; *DVD*: *Region 1*: Universal, May 2004, 2.35:1; *Region 2*: NA.

Premise: A man's wife drives him to extremes of behavior

"I can't afford a fucking dream house!" screams Nicholson's Charlie Smith in this tale set along the Texas–Mexico border, and that just about explains it all; what could have been interesting about this film, and what it is really about. *The Border* came out at a time when illegal immigrants were suddenly vexing American citizens. Smith is a border patrol officer stuck with a materialist, acquisitive, demanding wife (Perrine). Although it is *kind* of a crime story and is set in premiere soleil territory, the film only hints at film soleil components and the filmmakers are more concerned with their easy, lazy critique of American excess than with establishing a fully realised, interesting, unpredictable plot.

La Balance *Director*: Bob Swaim; *Writer*: Swaim, with M. Fabiani; *Key Cast*: Nathalie Baye (Nicole Danet), Philippe Léotard (Dédé Laffont), Richard Berry (Mathias Palouzi); *Cinematography*: Bernard Zitzermann; *Music*: Roland Bocquet; *Studio/Distributor*: Quartet (USA); *Running Time*: 103 minutes; *Release Date*: 10 November, 1982, France;

Rating: R; *DVD*: *Region 1*: HVE, 2004, 1.66:1, with trailer, filmography; *Region 2*: NA.

Premise: Cops use a pimp and his whore to get at a gang kingpin

Though festooned with posters of tough movie cops, such as Clint Eastwood and Steve McQueen, the offices of the special task force based in Belleville house men who have no code of honor. In the course of this tale the cops betray their snitches, mess up nearly every operation, and, in the end, even summarily execute one suspect with impunity. Yet overall the film pretends, with thinly veiled contempt, that these men are doing good. From today's perspective they are little better than the thugs they chase, a common enough trope in noir, neo-noir, and soleil, as is the climactic chase through the city, a standard last movement from *Naked City* to *The French Connection*. The heart of the film belongs to Baye's hooker and her pimp-lover Leotard (looking like the physical embodiment of Dick Tracy's Mumbles). They are blackmailed by the cops into betraying a crime kingpin ("Every time a hood gets bumped they say he's a stoolie," laments Baye, defining the slang of the film's title). There is a lovely scene introducing them in which the duo spar, flirt, argue, and discuss domestic chores, evincing a cozy intimacy that both the cops and the crooks are denied. In the end she betrays him to save him, the reverse of Patricia in *A Bout de Soufflé*. The cops think this is a happy ending. It isn't.

1983

✸ **Breathless**; *Director:* Jim McBride; *Writer:* McBride and L. M. Kit Carson, from Godard's film; *Key Cast:* Richard Gere (Jesse Lujack), Valérie Kaprisky (Monica Poiccard); *Cinematography:* Richard H. Kline; *Music:* Jack Nitzsche; *Studio/Distributor:* Orion; *Running Time:* 97 minutes; *Release Date:* 1983, USA; *Rating:* R; *DVD:* Region 1: MGM, April 2001, full frame; *Region 2:* MGM, March, 2001, 1.85:1.

Premise: Similar to the Godard film

To closed-minded middle brow critics of the time the notion of remaking Godard's groundbreaking *À Bout de Souffle*, arguably one of the most influential films of the 1960s, was outrageous, impossible, comical, embarrassing. The subsequent film, however, did not fuel much in the way of further debate or outrage. However, it did have an influence on Quentin Tarantino, who appears to have been smitten with Gere's jittery Jesse, the hyperactive, ceaselessly verbal hoodlum (the line from a Jerry Lee Lewis song, "Can't stop, won't stop, never stop," is his motto) who, as in Godard's film, kills a cop and tries to seduce a foreign girl. McBride flips the American girl in Paris for a French architecture student in Los Angeles, and exchanges Belmondo's obsession with Bogart with Jesse's fixation on Jack Kirby's Marvel comic book hero the Silver Surfer. From the Surfer to the obvious back projected car rides, and from the film's surf music track to Jesse's remark in a swimming pool that toes are a very important feature on a woman, one can see how Tarantino would have liked *Breathless*. The remake is surprisingly close to the original in narrative arc, although without the trend-setting stylistic bravura, even to the point of including a 20-minute sequence of anger, flirtation, pregnancy, lit crit discussion and sex between Jesse and Monica in her apartment; in other words it adapts Godard the writer without adopting Godard the stylist. It's as if the story were the *most* important thing in Godard's film. On the other hand, McBride and Carson find an eternal purity or innocence in the film's simple narrative. Like a Thompson novel, it contrasts weak men with strong men, and ends with a Thompsonian race to the Mexican border.

Scarface; *Director*: Brian De Palma; *Writer:* Oliver Stone, from the Ben Hecht-Howard Hawks film, based on a book by Armitage Trail; *Key Cast*: Al Pacino (Tony Montana), Steven Bauer (Manny Ribera), Michelle Pfeiffer (Elvira); *Cinematography*: John A. Alonzo; *Music*: Giorgio Moroder; *Studio/Distributor*: Universal; *Running Time*: 170 minutes; *Release Date*: 9 December, 1983, USA; *Rating*: R; *DVD*: *Region 1*: Universal, September 2003, 2.35:1, with several making ofs, deleted scenes; *Region 2*: Universal, January, 2001.

Premise: The rise and fall of a Cuban gangster in America

Scarface is not just a modernisation of Howard Hawks' 1932 gangster epic, but an interesting variation on Brian De Palma's common, obsessive theme. Almost all of De Palma's films are about a man betraying his closest friend. And not just betraying him, but fucking the friend over in the most grotesque and evil manner (from *Obsession* to *Snake Eyes*). Usually, De Palma invests the betrayed with all his emotional support. Here, De Palma takes you into the betrayer's mind. Pacino plays (overplays?) a monster, but rarely has De Palma actually investigated the evil side of his tales so closely. He's a riveting character and you see Tony's descendants in such films as *City of God* (Meirelles and Lund, 2002), whose psychopath out-Tonys Montana in his utter lack of feeling or loyalty for other people. Also interesting is Oliver Stone's contribution as writer at this early stage of his career. He was still the Oscar-winning wild man of screenwriting, not taken entirely seriously, and not known so much as a director. Yet in a few short years he goes from screenwriter to cinema god. What made the difference? What did he have that other struggling writer-directors didn't? Only insiders know. I guess it is a sign of how much we diminish the importance of writers, indeed will *always* diminish them, before the incense-scented shrine of the Director.

1984

Against All Odds; *Director*: Taylor Hackford; *Writer*: Eric Hughes, from the 1947 film *Out of the Past*; *Key Cast*: Rachel Ward (Jessie Wyler), Jeff Bridges (Terry Brogan), James Woods (Jake Wise); *Cinematography*: Donald E. Thorin; *Music*: Larry Carlton; *Studio/Distributor*: Columbia; *Running Time*: 128 minutes; *Release Date*: 2 March, 1984, USA; *Rating*: R; *DVD*: *Region 1*: Columbia, December 1999, 1.85:1, with filmmaker commentary, actor commentary, music videos, deleted scenes; *Region 2*: NA.

Premise: A gambler hires an ex-football player to retrieve his girlfriend

Supposedly a remake of *Out of the Past*, the modern film has very little in common with its ancestor except the bare bones of the premise, in which a gambler sends a man to fetch his runaway girlfriend, only to find that his employee has started an affair with her. But this lengthy modernisation is much more complex, layering incident upon incident, social observation upon outrage. As Joe Bob Briggs would say, there is a whole lotta plot here getting in the way of the story. Still, Rachel Ward anticipates other soleil heroines in her single-minded greed and selfishness.

✳ *The Hit*; *Director*: Stephen Frears; *Writer*: Peter Prince; *Key Cast*: John Hurt (Braddock), Terence Stamp (Willie Parker), Tim Roth (Myron), Laura del Sol (Maggie); *Cinematography*: Mike Molloy; *Music*: Paco de Lucia; *Studio/Distributor*: Island; *Running Time*: 100 minutes; *Release Date*: September, 1984; *Rating*: R; *DVD*: *Region 1*: Artisan, November 2002, full frame; *Region 2*: EuroVideo, November 1999.

Premise: Two enforcers track down a gangster hiding out in Spain

Ultimately more of a travelogue, or a tale of men out of their element, *The Hit* was the long anticipated follow up to Frears' cult hit *Gumshoe* (1971). In the interim he became one of the key British television directors of the 1970s. If *The Hit* ultimately proves to be rather lightweight in the face of such anticipation, it may be because the title and the premise mislead the viewer as to the film's real concerns (displacement, alienation). Hurt and Roth's hit men also anticipate, in some ways, the killer duos of Tarantino's later films, and the tale has some of the same tone as *Sexy Beast* (2000).

1985

✳ *Blood Simple*; *Director:* Joel Coen; *Writer:* The Coens; *Key Cast:* John Getz (Ray), Frances McDormand (Abby), Dan Hedaya (Julian Marty), M. Emmet Walsh (Loren Visser); *Cinematography:* Barry Sonnenfeld; *Music:* Carter Burwell; *Studio/Distributor:* Circle Films; *Running Time:* 99 minutes; *Release Date:* 18 January, 1985, USA (though it played at the Toronto Film Festival the previous autumn); *Rating:* R; *DVD:* *Region 1:* Universal, September 2001, 1.85:1, with commentary; *Region 2:* NA.

Premise: A love triangle turns deadly

With *Blood Simple*, not only were two fantastic new talents boldly announcing themselves (the Coen Brothers), but a whole new genre, film soleil, finally came into its own. Also, in its weird, if stylish, low-budget way, *Blood Simple* is one of the best adaptations of the spirit of James M. Cain and Jim Thompson, whose influence hovers over all film soleils. Its characters are stupid. One mistakes another for a murderer; a third thinks that a dead man has come back to life. These stupid people bump into each other and miscommunicate like the brutal people in Scorsese movies such as *Taxi Driver*. Yet they are also surprisingly, poetically articulate: "Now in Russia, they got it all mapped out so that everyone pulls for everyone else. That's the theory anyway. But what I know about is Texas, and down here… you're on your own."

✳ *To Live and Die in L.A*; *Director:* William Friedkin; *Writer:* Friedkin and Gerald Petievich, from his novel; *Key Cast:* William L. Petersen (Richard Chance), Willem Dafoe (Rick

Masters), John Pankow (John Vukovich); *Cinematography*: Robby Muller, Robert D. Yeoman; *Music*: Wang Chung; *Studio/Distributor:* MGM; *Running Time*: 116 minutes; *Release Date*: 1 November, 1985, USA; *Rating*: R; *DVD*: *Region 1*: MGM, December 2003, 1.85:1, with director commentary, deleted scenes, making of; *Region 2*: MGM, October, 2004.

Premise: A driven Treasury agent is after a brilliant counterfeiter

To Live and Die is something like the third or fourth underrated William Friedkin film, after *Sorcerer* (see page 85) and *Rampage* (1988). The public supposedly found nothing of interest in any of them, and the films floundered at the box office. *To Live and Die* is filled with great actors, great scenes, and a disturbing portrayal of crime fighting, one of the last films to take a sour and depressing view of that enterprise. It was the first lead role by William Petersen, a subsequently underused actor who has found a measure of richly deserved success on TV with *CSI*. It was the third or fourth film with Willem Dafoe, now a major art house actor and character actor in mainstream movies. John Pankow went on to a part in American Sitcoms. John Turturro became an indie favorite and key element in the Coen Brothers' movies. Dean Stockwell offers a subtly brilliant turn as a lawyer. Robby Muller beautifully photographs the film, and Robert Yeoman, who has gone on to do several important movies, shot the second unit car chase. Wang Chung did the catchy soundtrack. The premise of *To Live and Die* is somewhat typical of 1980s action films, about a Treasury agent named Chance (Petersen) out to get the counterfeiter who killed his partner. The paper man is a former convict and faux artist named Rick Masters (Dafoe), who seems in despair about the fact that he is a better counterfeiter than he is a painter. The Treasury has tried to get to him several times with no success, but Chance will let nothing stand in his way. After a series of machinations, Chance and his new partner, John Vukovich (Pankow) get access to Masters. But of course things go awry. *To Live and Die* is different from any other Los Angeles film you have seen. It's not the Los Angeles of Rodeo Drive and Hollywood and palm trees. It's the industrial LA of oilrigs and warehouses and docks and huge tanks sitting near the water, and the smell of industry rising over a bleak city. It is a world of perpetual sunset, where the purple sky mocks the pallid faces of the driven, desperate people all hustling each other. Counterfeit money is the prime mover, and all the people in the film are counterfeit. All the women are playing the men. All the underlings are faking out their bosses. No one's identity is real. Into this swirling whirlpool of falsity and unreality, Chance is trying to right a wrong, and Vukovich is trying to keep his head on straight. It's hard when Chance drives him 100 miles an hour the wrong way down a freeway in a harebrained scheme to raise some quick cash.

1986

✻ ***Manhunter***; *Director*: Michael Mann; *Writer:* Mann, from the Thomas Harris novel *Red Dragon*; *Key Cast*: William Petersen (Will Graham), Kim Greist (Molly Graham), Joan Allen (Reba McClane), Brian Cox (Dr. Hannibal Lecktor), Dennis Farina (Jack Crawford), Tom Noonan (Francis Dollarhyde); *Cinematography*: Dante Spinotti; *Music*: Michel Rubini and Klaus Schulze; *Studio/Distributor*: DEG; *Running*

Time: 119 minutes; *Release Date*: 15 August, 1986, USA; *Rating*: R; *DVD*: *Region 1*: two by Anchor Bay, the most recent, July 2003, 2.35:1, with director commentary, deleted scenes, stills, posters, script; *Region 2*: Kinowelt, August 2001, with making ofs, stills.

Premise: A former FBI man is pulled back in to find a serial killer

There is something almost mystical about the way Michael Mann can get his actors to *move* in a certain manner. Like the way Daniel Day Lewis' hair sways when he runs through the woods in *The Last of the Mohicans* (1992). Or the way Russell Crowe pushes his glasses up with his forefinger in *The Insider* (1999). *Manhunter*, the first version of Thomas Harris' book *Red Dragon*, is full of such moments, like the way William Petersen puts a clue in a plastic sack while pivoting to look up a tree. Michael Mann worked on the script for this film for three years, and it shows. It is stripped down (Thomas Harris fans would say too stripped), subtle, and leaves lots of room for great visuals and interesting interpretations. Mann was just about to go on and take over television with his neo-noir film soleil series *Miami Vice*, and you see the roots of that show's look in this movie. The film is also what Mann calls the "first iteration" of Hannibal Lecter (his name spelled differently in this movie). He is not the attractive figure of later films. Brian Cox does a brilliant job at showing Lecter as both charming and cunning, and yet also unsocialised. Mann is one of the most consistent soleil-oriented directors (like the Coens and John Dahl). *Manhunter* is gorgeous, funny, cruel and powerful.

1987

Slam Dance; *Director:* Wayne Wang; *Writer:* Don Opper; *Key Cast:* Virginia Madsen (Yolanda Caldwell), Tom Hulce (C. C. Drood), Mary Elizabeth Mastrantonio (Helen Drood); *Cinematography:* Amir M. Mokri; *Music:* Mitchell Froom; *Studio/Distributor:* Island; *Running Time:* 100 minutes; *Release Date:* 6 November 1987, USA; *Rating:* R; *DVD:* NA.

Premise: A cartoonist is the chief suspect when a mysterious woman is murdered

The year 1987 was something of an annus mirabilis for film soleil (as later, was 1990). Along with *Slam Dance*, that year saw the release of *Siesta*, *The Big Easy*, *Extreme Prejudice*, *Black Widow*, *Raising Arizona*, and *Best Seller*, all of which qualify in some ways as film soleil, or have soleil elements. If one chooses *Slam Dance* to represent this year it's because Wang's film has the most links with past noir (it's a variation of a femme fatale/innocent man on the run story) and the soleil elements that would figure in later films of its kind. On the surface *Slam Dance* seems like a love story, only one half of the relationship is dead (Virginia Madsen). In reality, the spirit of the film rests in the banter between the cop investigating her death (Harry Dean Stanton) and the man he suspects of murdering her (Hulce). Sadly, although it is of interest, *Slam Dance* doesn't really work, mostly because it allows whatever tension might reside in the story to dissipate at the expense of exploring tangential quirky characters in a misguided attempt to seem "Altmanian."

1988

DOA; *Director*: Rocky Morton and Annabel Jankel; *Writer*: Charles Edward Pogue; *Key Cast*: Dennis Quaid (Dexter Cornell), Meg Ryan (Sydney Fuller), Charlotte Rampling (Mrs. Fitzwaring); *Cinematography*: Yuri Neyman; *Music*: Chaz Jankel; *Studio/Distributor*: Touchstone; *Running Time*: 96 minutes; *Release Date*: 18 March 1988, USA; *Rating*: R; *DVD*: *Region 1*: NA; *Region 2*: Touchstone, December 2002, 1.85:1.

Premise: A college professor tries to find the person who has given him a slow acting poison

Hollywood has always "remade" movies of the past, but in the mass of remakes that surfaced in the 1980s, this brighter version of the dark noir from 1950, originally starring Edmond O'Brien, took some unusual turns. Co-directed by the creators of TV's *Max Headroom*, this *DOA* is set in an academic milieu (the University of Texas, in Austin), and drops most of the material from the first film but for the essential concept: that a man has been poisoned, and has 24 hours in which to find his killer (while being suspected of murder himself). Morton and Jankel bring visual verve to the story, and the idea of academic jealousy as a motivating force in a plot (in some respects resembling the future *Wonder Boys*, 2000), but unfortunately Quaid is not entirely convincing as an academic and the plot is unduly murky and tangent-filled.

1989

✴ **Dead Calm**; *Director*: Philip Noyce; *Writer*: Terry Hayes, from the Charles Williams novel; *Key Cast*: Nicole Kidman

(*Rae Ingram*), Sam Neill (*John Ingram*), Billy Zane (*Hughie Warriner*); *Cinematography*: Dean Sempler, with Geoff Burton; *Music*: Graeme Revell; *Studio/Distributor*: Warner; *Running Time*: 96 minutes; *Release Date*: 7 April 1989, USA; *Rating*: R; *DVD*: *Region 1*: Warner, December 1999, 2.35:1; *Region 2*: Warner, February 2000.

Premise: A psychotic man overtakes a couple yachting

Orson Welles attempted to film Charles Williams' novel *Dead Calm,* as *The Deep* in the early 1970s, but left it unfinished and unreleased. In the absence of that potential masterpiece came Philip Noyce's taut, efficient thriller, produced by George Miller (*Mad Max*). It is easily Noyce's best film. And *Dead Calm* happened to introduce Nicole Kidman to a world audience. There are some who still prefer this tougher early version of the Kidman persona, with her spear gun and sports watch, to the more sophisticated public figure, all porcelain chilliness. Zane's villain is like a demon summoned from the unconscious to test the marriage of Naval doctor Neill and his bride, who recently lost their son. Noyce and company do an exquisite job of ratcheting the suspense and heightening sympathy for the separated couple, who can and must do anything to reunite. The Brando-esque Zane, however, is simply a force of evil, a virus moving from host to host, nearly unstoppable in the convention of post-teen slasher films, leading to a very last few minutes of the film that are something of a disappointment (but then, they are in most movies).

Kill Me Again; *Director*: John Dahl; *Writer:* Dahl, and David W. Warfield; *Key Cast*: Michael Madsen (Vince Miller),

Joanne Whalley-Kilmer (Fay Forrester), Val Kilmer (Jack Andrews); *Cinematography*: Jacques Steyn; *Music*: William Olvis; *Studio/Distributor:* Propaganda; *Running Time*: 94 minutes; *Release Date*: 27 October 1989, USA; *Rating*: R; *DVD*: *Region 1*: MGM, December 2000, pan and scan; *Region 2*: NA.

Premise: A woman asks a PI to fake her death

Kill Me Again begins with the classic private eye set-up. A glamorous, mysterious, alluring woman seeks out a down-on-his-heels detective. In this case, the woman has a strange request: her own death (it's somewhat similar to *Lady from Shanghai*). The detective is consequently embroiled in a complex caper beyond his intellectual capabilities, and pitted against a more brutal adversary (Madsen's Vince). For whatever reason (failure of conception, budgetary issues) the film is more ambitious than successful, but it does employ pleasing visual echoes of earlier noir films. The headstrong, cunning Fay anticipates Dahl's later femme fatales, especially Fiorentino's Bridget Gregory in *The Last Seduction*.

Additional, Potential, or Honorary Films Soleils: 1980: *The Long Good Friday, Union City, Atlantic City*; 1981: *Eyewitness, Thief, Diva*; 1984: *Once Upon a Time in America*; 1986: *Eight Million Ways to Die, No Mercy, 52 Pick Up*; 1987: *Siesta, The Big Easy, Extreme Prejudice, Black Widow, Raising Arizona, Best Seller*; 1988: *Cop, Tequila Sunrise, Masquerade*; 1989: *Monsieur Hire, The Kill-Off*.

The 1990s

It's a decade that will go down in cinematic history as famous for its film soleil. It's soleil's *decadus mirabilis*. If the 1980s were defined by Reagan's ascendancy and its political and cinematic ramifications, then Bill Clinton's seemingly benign stewardship over newfound wealth unleashed a disquieting series of movies that mix greed and murder in tableaux that undermine one's security about the shape of the world.

1990

Internal Affairs; *Director:* Mike Figgis; *Writer:* Henry Bean; *Key Cast:* Richard Gere (Dennis Peck), Andy Garcia (Raymond Avilla), Nancy Travis (Kathleen Avilla), Laurie Metcalf (Amy Wallace); *Cinematography:* John A. Alonzo; *Music:* Brian Banks, Mike Figgis, Anthony Marinelli; *Studio/Distributor:* Paramount; *Running Time:* 115 minutes; *Release Date:* 12 January 1990, USA; *Rating:* R; *DVD: Region 1:* Paramount, March 1999, 1.85:1; *Region 2:* Paramount, March 2001.

Premise: An internal affairs cop bucks up against his corrupt prey

In a twist typical of film soleil, the villain of this piece is both a cop and much more certain of his belief system and goals than the ostensible hero. After a terrific beginning and an intriguing portrayal of Gere's bad cop (the worst until *Training Day*), the ending proves perfunctory.

Impulse; *Director:* Sondra Locke; *Writer:* John DeMarco and Leigh Chapman; *Key Cast:* Theresa Russell (Lottie Mason), Jeff Fahey (Stan), George Dzundza (Lt. Joe Morgan); *Cinematography:* Dean Semler; *Music:* Michel Colombier; *Studio/Distributor:* Warner; *Running Time:* 109 minutes; *Release Date:* 6 April 1990, USA; *Rating:* R; *DVD:* NA.

Premise: A female vice cop is living on the edge

A fascinating, obscure movie that ended up going straight to video, *Impulse* (a typical Hollywood non-title, a label that says nothing) explores the troubled cop angle from the female perspective. *Impulse* isn't the first film to do so, but it is the best. Russell is brilliant and seductive as an undercover cop pulled in numerous directions and sought out by numerous men (and as in the later *Basic Instinct* she's a cop who must see a shrink). She's almost schizophrenic, bouncing between her "real" life and her undercover life, and the movie orchestrates every facet to buttress its presentation of her (she even wears two watches, a fashion watch when she's "feminine" and a sports watch when she's a cop). Although the film eventually settles for a simple whodunit fourth act to resolve the plot thread of which man in her life is her stalker, until then *Impulse* is a gripping character study.

Miami Blues; *Director:* George Armitage; *Writer:* Armitage, from Charles Willeford's novel; *Key Cast:* Alec Baldwin (Frederick J. Frenger Jr.), Fred Ward (Sgt. Hoke Moseley); *Cinematography:* Tak Fujimoto; *Music:* Gary Chang; *Studio/Distributor:* Orion; *Running Time:* 97 minutes; *Release Date:* 20 April 1990, USA; *Rating:* R; *DVD: Region 1:* MGM, December 2002, 1.85:1; *Region 2:* NA.

Premise: A cop dedicates himself to ending the crime spree of a sociopath

"He got your gun, your badge, and your teeth? You are a disgrace to the police force." Well, yes, sociopath Frenger did end up with cop Hoke Moseley's gun, badge and teeth, but the tenacious Moseley gets them all back. Set in what has come to be called Elmore Leonard country – southern Florida – *Miami Blues* takes a more comical stance to its subject matter than that found in Charles Willeford's source novel, as if the filmmakers *were* adapting a Leonard book. However, the subtly brilliant acting from Baldwin, Ward, and others makes up for this skewed take.

❋ *Wild at Heart* [*David Lynch's Wild at Heart*]; *Director:* David Lynch; *Writer:* Lynch, from Barry Gifford's novel *Wild at Heart: The Story of Sailor and Lula*; *Key Cast:* Nicolas Cage (Sailor Ripley), Laura Dern (Lula Pace), Willem Dafoe (Bobby Peru); *Cinematography:* Frederick Elmes; *Music:* Angelo Badalamenti; *Studio/Distributor:* Propaganda; *Running Time:* 124 minutes; *Release Date:* 17 August 1990, USA; *Rating:* R; *DVD: Region 1:* MGM, December 2004, 2.35:1, with making of, director interview, interviews, stills, commercials; *Region 2:* NA.

Premise: Two young lovers hit the road with several nemeses in pursuit

"This whole world's wild at heart and weird on top." That about sums up David Lynch's film as well. A simultaneous trip through Hell and Oz, it's a bridge between *Bonnie and Clyde* and *True Romance* – or *Natural Born Killers.* A parody that wants to be taken seriously and a pulp story with artistic pretentious, a spit in the face of the audience and a tiger purring for attention, *Wild at Heart* is all things to all viewers. As episodic as any lovers-on-the-road film, it also embraces a comical sense of violence unseen since Lynch's first film, *Eraserhead*. The film also juxtaposes Lynch's usual dichotomy of shrill older evildoers versus innocent young lovers. Personally, I dislike it, but still it remains a key entry in the burgeoning advent of film soleil.

✳ *After Dark, My Sweet*; *Director:* James Foley; *Writer:* Foley and Robert Redlin from the novel by Jim Thompson; *Key Cast*: Jason Patric (Kevin 'Kid' Collins), Rachel Ward (Fay Anderson), Bruce Dern (Uncle Bud); *Cinematography*: Mark Plummer; *Music*: Maurice Jarre; *Studio/Distributor:* Avenue; *Running Time*: 114 minutes; *Release Date*: 24 August 1990, USA; *Rating*: R; *DVD*: *Region 1*: Artisan, March 2002, 1.85:1; *Region 2*: NA.

Premise: An ex-boxer drifts into a kidnapping scheme

Rachel Ward had the potential of becoming *the* femme fatale of film soleil. But she appears to have mostly retired from cinema shortly after making this film for soleil specialist James Foley. But she is not alone in riveting the attention of the viewer in this film. Dern and Patric, both superb, join her. As a Thompson adaptation, *After Dark* features the typical Thompson hero, half crazy and wholly underestimated by those around him. This quiet masterpiece begins simply but builds in complexity, almost to the last few seconds. With some qualifications, *After Dark* isolates the essence of film soleil.

✳ *The Hot Spot*; *Director:* Dennis Hopper; *Writer:* Nona Tyson and Charles Williams, from Williams' novel; *Key Cast*: Don Johnson (Harry Madox), Virginia Madsen (Dolly Harshaw), Jennifer Connelly (Gloria Harper); *Cinematography*: Ueli Steiger; *Music*: Jack Nitzsche; *Studio/Distributor:* Orion; *Running Time*: 130 minutes; *Release Date*: 12 October 1990, USA; *Rating*: R; *DVD*: NA.

Premise: A drifter's bank heist plan leads to enslavement by two women

Given that *The Hot Spot* stars a popular male sex symbol, it's interesting to compare it to Clint Eastwood projects such as *The Beguiled* and to Eastwood's directorial debut *Play Misty For Me*. All these films, woven around a top male box office draw, take a rather narrow, suspicious, frightened view of women, a view that can be confused as a breakthrough for the feminist revolution, if you think that making women killers on par with men suffices as a breakthrough. It's suppose to be politically cool that Don Johnson's Harry, drifting into town to do a bank heist only to end up the sexual slave of two women, is victimised by self-assertive women who know what they want. As in many a film soleil, the women end up on top. In soleil, the femme fatale is *not* required, by codes or convention, to end on a bad note in order to appease the prevailing morality. Under Hopper's direction, however, *The Hot Spot* avoids any hint of the soapbox by making its women witty in their greed and by capturing a lazy, catty 1950s mood rather than a robust, aggressive 1990s one.

✳ *The Grifters*; *Director:* Stephen Frears; *Writer:* Donald E. Westlake from the Jim Thompson novel; *Key Cast*: Anjelica

Huston (Lilly Dillon), John Cusack (Roy Dillon), Annette Bening (Myra Langtry); *Cinematography*: Oliver Stapleton; *Music*: Elmer Bernstein; *Studio/Distributor:* Miramax; *Running Time*: 119 minutes; *Release Date*: 5 December 1990, USA; *Rating*: R; *DVD*: *Region 1*: Miramax, September 2002, 1.85:1, with director, actor, and writer commentary, making of, stills, novelist documentary; *Region 2*: NA.

Premise: The lives of three related con artists go awry

Director Frears returns to film soleil in this Thompson adaptation that is from one of the author's bleakest tales. An excellent cast does an excellent job, with meaty roles that includes dialogue such as "One question. Do you want to stick to that story, or do you want to keep your teeth?" Frears maintains the integrity of the story's bittersweet climax.

1991

Thelma & Louise; *Director*: Ridley Scott; *Writer:* Callie Khouri; *Key Cast*: Susan Sarandon (Louise), Geena Davis (Thelma), Harvey Keitel (Hal), Michael Madsen (Jimmy), Christopher McDonald (Darryl), Brad Pitt (J.D.); *Cinematography*: Adrian Biddle; *Music*: Hans Zimmer; *Studio/Distributor:* MGM; *Running Time*: 129 minutes; *Release Date*: 24 May 1991, USA; *Rating*: R; *DVD*: *Region 1*: MGM, February 2003, 2.35:1, with director commentary, cast and writer commentary, alternate ending, extended and deleted scenes, making of, storyboards, music video; *Region 2*: MGM, September 1998, with director commentary and alternate ending (the R2 transfer is reputedly better than the R1).

Premise: A short trip turns into a police pursuit for two friends

Thelma & Louise was almost more of a sociological event, a rallying cry, an excuse for pundits to excoriate the decline of western civilisation than it was a mere movie. To re-view it after a long hiatus is to be reminded how funny it is at its root, (especially Christopher McDonald as Thelma's husband Darryl), how beautifully shot it is (by Adrian Biddle), and how evocative the music is (by Ridley Scott regular Hans Zimmer). In its tale of two lower class girls on a brief vacation who end up hunted by the law, Geena Davis' performance is terribly underrated; especially good is a short scene in which Thelma talks about "crossing a line" in her mind. The mixture of wonder, realisation, and fear on her face is priceless. The film constitutes a variation of soleil in having two girls on the road and on the run, but its southwestern setting was becoming very familiar to close observes. *Thelma & Louise* is a great film, and today the aspects that seemed off-putting, such as the parody of a sexist pig whose oil truck the girls blow up, feel less problematic. The supplementary material on the latest DVD also makes clear what a collaborative effort the whole thing proved to be and, for example, the oil truck scene would have been worse, we learn, if Sarandon hadn't insisted on some changes.

❋ ***Delusion***; *Director:* Carl Colpaert; *Writer:* Colpaert with Kurt Voss; *Key Cast:* Jim Metzler (George O'Brien), Jennifer Rubin (Patti), Kyle Secor (Chevy), Jerry Orbach (Larry); *Cinematography:* Geza Sinkovics; *Music:* Barry Adamson; *Studio/Distributor:* Cineville; *Running Time:* 88 minutes; *Release Date:* 7 June 1991, USA; *Rating:* R; *DVD:* NA.

Premise: Three volatile people meet in the desert

Set against the same specific bleak desert landscape as *Kill Me Again* and *Sidney*, Copeart's thriller is soleil crossed with a measure of an old west showdown between good and evil, as it tells of a disgruntled dotcom executive who has embezzled large sums from the company he used to work for (a victim of a takeover) who picks up a strange couple on the road whose car has overturned. As in *Red Rock West* and in most hijack road movies, there is a hit man, a beautiful woman, and a victim, whose dance of death is interrupted in this case by the alien integer of the dotcom crook. In most "kidnapper" vehicles, the innocent bystander is truly innocent; in modern soleil, he is usually only a shade more honest then his captors, a morally compromised figure whom the filmmakers make it difficult for us to identify with (unless we are honest with ourselves about our own general failings). One obvious question is why the film is called "delusion"? One delusion is that O'Brien will be able to effortlessly use his stolen loot to start his new company. But Secor's Chevy is also delusional: he is playing more a fantasy of a hit man than the real thing (in this way also anticipating the role playing themes of Tarantino's films, especially *Pulp Fiction*). Copeart, a Belgian filmmaker, many of whose American films have desert settings, has here made a film with all the earmarks of what would become an indie staple: small cast, low budget, crime story used as a vehicle for a larger sociological statement.

1992

✴ *Reservoir Dogs*; *Director:* Quentin Tarantino; *Writer:* Tarantino; *Key Cast:* Harvey Keitel (Mr. White/Larry

Dimmick), Tim Roth (Mr. Orange/Freddy Newandyke), Michael Madsen (Mr. Blonde/Vic Vega), Steve Buscemi (Mr. Pink); *Cinematography*: Andrzej Sekula; *Music*: Carefully selected pop tunes; *Studio/Distributor*: Live; *Running Time*: 99 minutes; *Release Date*: 21 January 1992 *(Sundance Film Festival)*; *Rating*: R; *DVD*: *Region 1*: Artisan, August 2002, 2.35:1, with ear scene alternate footage, workshop footage, Sundance feature, cast and crew interviews, Lawrence Tierney feature, influences feature, film noir influence feature, real criminals feature, action figure feature, scholars audio commentary, K-BILLY feature, location feature, poster gallery, and deleted scenes (which highlight what would have been the finished film's only major female role); *Region 2*: Momentum, November 2000, with Tarantino intro.

Premise: A diamond heist goes awry

What we forget, more than 10 years after his debut feature, is that Quentin Tarantino started out as a would-be actor. The mythology of the video store clerk turned movie director belies the previous decade that he spent thinking of himself as an actor, taking lessons, doing scenes, trying to get parts. His first film is therefore infused with actorial insights. *Reservoir Dogs* is about interpretation. The interpretive arts are employed at every single significant point in the narrative, and during most of the 'insignificant' ones, too. The movie begins with a guy explaining the meaning of Madonna's *Like a Virgin*. It ends with a gangster realising that he had failed to interpret reality correctly. But interpretation as the *modus vivendi* in the film is established in the opening scene. Joe Cabot (Lawrence Tierney), the organiser of the heist, is obsessed with an old telephone book he found in a coat pocket, going over the names again and again, trying to remember the people, to the irritation of Mr. White. Also there is the anti-tipper (Steve Buscemi's Mr. Pink) who needs to (futilely) explain that his refusal to tip is based on his analysis of a waiter's *performance*. Finished with their meal, the black-garbed crew exit to participate in a heist that they fail to 'read' right. Throughout the movie there are 'interpretive' moments. Mr. Pink analyses why his name isn't as cool as the others. The surviving gang members re-group and try to read back through recent events in order to figure out who is the snitch. But in the biggest component of the story, a man must make sure that he is *not* interpreted. Mr. Orange (Tim Roth) needs to pass under the radar of the crew's scrutiny. That's because he is an undercover cop named Freddy Newendyke, whose success at burrowing into the gang is dependent on his presenting a 'character' whom the other men can buy into without hesitation. To do this, he must be trained by an experienced undercover man (the restless Randy Brooks), who gives the cop pointers in 'reading' his auditors. As Mr. Orange delivers an 'audition' monologue about a tense but imaginary incident involving pot and a train station bathroom full of cops, the movie interprets the 'amusing anecdote' *for* us, casting and directing it, creating the 'movie' that the gangsters might see in their minds. And dare one add that 'theft,' too, is an interpretive act? Not just the theft of jewels, but also the theft of other movies to bulk out one's own? What Tarantino did with *Reservoir Dogs,* in a script credited solely to him, was to borrow or pay *hommage* to a number of films (*City on Fire, A Clockwork Orange, The Taking of Pelham One Two Three, The Killing*) that augment or support his own project. Conscious or not, the theme of actorial interpretation is so consistently woven throughout the movie that it gives the film a sustaining, cohesive meta-text. Part of the tale's tragedy is that the one guy who needs to understand reality the most, Keitel's Mr. White (real name: Lawrence Dimick; like many actors, they all have stage names), is the one who can't interpret the truth. He lets himself be swayed by personal feelings.

White Sands; *Director:* Roger Donaldson; *Writer:* Daniel Pyne; *Key Cast:* Willem Dafoe (Deputy Sheriff Ray Dolezal), Mary Elizabeth Mastrantonio (Lane Bodine), Mickey Rourke (Gorman Lennox); *Cinematography:* Peter Menzies Jr.; *Music:* Patrick O'Hearn; *Studio/Distributor:* Warner; *Running Time:* 101 minutes; *Release Date:* 24 April 1992, USA; *Rating:* R; *DVD: Region 1:* Warner, July 2000, 2.35:1; *Region 2:* NA.

Premise: A sheriff stumbles into an FBI case

It's hard to tell how this film went wrong, if it was bad casting, or a bad script (which gets increasingly bizarre as it goes along), or non-commanding direction (by Donaldson, who earlier did the dynamic *No Way Out*). In any case, this tale of a bored cop who goes undercover and discovers the dark night of his soul (in a plot that has echoes of the Schwarzenegger actioner *Raw Deal*) does enjoy some vivid visuals.

❋ One False Move; *Director:* Carl Franklin; *Writer:* Billy Bob Thornton and Tom Epperson; *Key Cast:* Bill Paxton (Chief Dale Dixon), Cynda Williams (Lila Walker), Billy Bob Thornton (Ray Malcolm); *Cinematography:* James L. Carter; *Music:* Peter Haycock, Derek Holt, and Terry Plumeri;

Studio/Distributor: Columbia; *Running Time*: 105 minutes; *Release Date*: 8 May 1992, USA; *Rating*: R; *DVD*: *Region 1*: Columbia, March 1999, 1.85:1, with director commentary; *Region 2*: Columbia, November 2000, same as R1.

Premise: Some small time crooks make a mysterious trek back to their Arkansas home town

What it lacks in visual distinction *One False Move* more than makes up for in the intensity and complexity of its performances. Such a film could easily be construed as actors slumming by playing characters from a scummier social class than the ones they are in or were born in, but here the cast digs into the script by credited writers Thornton and Epperson and in essence become the writers' best collaborators.

Guncrazy; *Director:* Tamra Davis; *Writer:* Matthew Bright; *Key Cast*: Drew Barrymore (Anita Minteer), James LeGros (Howard); *Cinematography*: Lisa Rinzler; *Music*: Ed Tomney; *Studio/Distributor:* First Look; *Running Time*: 97 minutes; *Release Date*: 11 September 1992, Toronto Film Festival; *Rating*: R; *DVD*: *Region 1*: First Look, May 2004, 1.78:1, with director commentary, star interview, making of, storyboards; *Region 2*: NA.

Premise: A high school girl and a killer hitch up

A blend of *Badlands* with the film's ostensive source, the Joseph H. Lewis' 1949 *Gun Crazy*, this low budget effort lacks the frenzy and hysteria of the latter or the intellectual distance of the former. Instead it embraces a sort of "mad love story" that echoes more *Bonnie and Clyde* (impotence is an issue here, too) and by coincidence movies such as Tarantino's *True Romance* and *Natural Born Killers*. In other words, seen as a love story the movie becomes both poignant and observant.

1993

✱ ***Red Rock West***; *Director:* John Dahl; *Writer:* Dahl and Rick Dahl; *Key Cast:* Nicolas Cage (Michael Williams), J.T. Walsh (Wayne Brown/Kevin McCord), Lara Flynn Boyle (Suzanne Brown/Ann McCord), Dennis Hopper (Lyle); *Cinematography:* Marc Reshovsky; *Music:* William Olvis; *Studio/Distributor:* Polygram; *Running Time:* 98 minutes; *Release Date:* 16 June 1993, France; *Rating:* R; *DVD: Region 1:* Columbia, August 1999, 1.85:1, with director commentary; *Region 2:* Columbia, August 2000.

Premise: Confused identities lead to chaos in a murder plot

Red Rock West is set in Wyoming and offers a variation on director Dahl's previous *Kill Me Again*. Here, a roaming, historyless man named Michael (Cage) arrives for a job at an oil field that he sabotages himself out of. His finances exhausted, Michael ends up in a bar in the town of Red Rock, whose owner Wayne (the late, great J.T. Walsh) thinks Michael is the hit man from Texas whom Wayne hired to kill his wife Suzanne (Boyle). Michael plays along for a while in order to get some money, but soon finds himself in over his head. The real hit man, Lyle (Hopper), finally arrives, other people turn out to be not who they seem, and Red Rock becomes a killing ground. Darker yet funnier than *Kill Me Again*, *Red Rock West* is more 'country' than desert (there's even a cameo appearance by country singer Dwight Yokum). It's a world of high neck beer bottles, truckstops and Stetsons. As a town, Red Rock is a noirish center of displacement. No one who lives there is supposed to be there or wants to be there. It's a place in which Suzanne, obsessed with horse riding, dons boots and jodhpurs more appropriate for a fox hunt than a gallop through a moisture-starved terrain, that fails to yield up the elegance and social position to which her garb suggests she aspires. It's a beautifully done film, and perhaps one of the five or six defining examples of film soleil.

Kalifornia; *Director:* Dominic Sena; *Writer:* Tim Metcalfe; *Key Cast:* Brad Pitt (Early Grayce), Juliette Lewis (Adele Corners), David Duchovny (Brian Kessler), Michelle Forbes (Carrie Laughlin); *Cinematography:* Bojan Bazelli; *Music:* Carter Burwell; *Studio/Distributor:* Gramercy; *Running Time:* 117 minutes; *Release Date:* 3 September 1993, USA; *Rating:* R; *DVD:* *Region 1:* MGM, August 2000, 1.85:1, with video interviews, B-roll; *Region 2:* NA.

Premise: An intellectual is used by a serial killer

Blessed with a pair of future superstars in its cast, *Kalifornia* blends a serial killer tale with film soleil road story. Critics at the time reviled the film for being more flash than substance (director Sena came from music videos, so the charge was stitched into virtually every review), and it's true that the opposition of ineffectual intellectual versus brute masculinity is a premise that has worn thin. However the vivacity of the stars inhabiting their roles and the sly humor sneaked into the horrific premise make the film a continuing interest. The climax, set in an old A-Bomb testing ground, renders the film a form of reply or response to Aldrich's *Kiss Me Deadly*.

Flesh and Bone; *Director*: Steve Kloves; *Writer*: Kloves; *Key Cast*: Dennis Quaid (Arlis Sweeney), James Caan (Roy Sweeney), Meg Ryan (Kay Davies), Gwyneth Paltrow (Ginnie); *Cinematography*: Philippe Rousselot; *Music*: Thomas Newman; *Studio/Distributor*: Paramount; *Running Time*: 126 minutes; *Release Date*: 5 November 1993, USA; *Rating*: R; *DVD*: *Region 1*: Paramount, April 2002, 1.85:1; *Region 2*: NA.

Premise: A dysfunctional family is haunted by a crime from the past

Something of a cult developed among the cinema cognoscenti for *Flesh and Bone* at the time of its release. Auteurists were interested in Kloves, who had made *The Fabulous Baker Boys* and would later write *Wonder Boys* and the Harry Potter films; the film was an interesting opportunity for prestige actresses such as Meg Ryan to act "down." And it introduced new talent while celebrating old standbys, such as Caan and character actor Scott Wilson. At the time of its release the film made back $6 million of its $9 million cost despite such critical regard. Does it hold up? Not really. It's still a fine film that suffers only from the irresolution built into the screenplay. Although well written, some of its finer bits get lost in the harsh splendor of the Texas landscape and the film's stately pace. Kloves obviously likes familial competition set within differing levels of dissipation. He clearly wants to tell a tale of fate coming back to reclaim people, but the languorous feel of the film, despite being born of the land the characters live in, works against the tone here.

1994

The Getaway; *Director:* Roger Donaldson; *Writer:* Walter Hill and Amy Jones; *Key Cast:* Alec Baldwin (Carter 'Doc' McCoy), Kim Basinger (Carol McCoy), Michael Madsen (Rudy Travis), James Woods (Jack Benyon); *Cinematography:* Peter Menzies Jr.; *Music:* Mark Isham; *Studio/Distributor:* Universal; *Running Time:* 115 minutes; *Release Date:* 11 February 1994, USA; *Rating:* R; *DVD: Region 1:* Universal, May 1998, 2.35:1, the unrated version; *Region 2:* NA.

Premise: Same as the 1972 film

Every generation, it seems, get *The Getaway* it deserves. And it happens when a movie star couple decides to celebrate their union with an action film in which they get to argue with each other and shoot people. This generation's stars the excellent Baldwin and Basinger in a film that is, like its predecessor, generous with supporting actors. A fuller, "hotter" version of the film was released to home video, taking advantage of the fact that Baldwin and Basinger were married at the time. Sadly, director Donaldson, though he has made some fine films, doesn't exude a firm personality of his own.

1995

❋ **Underneath**; *Director:* Steven Soderbergh; *Writer:* Soderbergh, from a previous script by Sam Lowry and Daniel Fuchs, from a novel by Don Tracy; *Key Cast:* Peter Gallagher (Michael Chambers), Alison Elliott (Rachel), William Fichtner (Tommy Dundee), Joe Don Baker (Clay Hinkle), Elisabeth Shue (Susan Crenshaw); *Cinematography:*

Elliot Davis; *Music*: Cliff Martinez; *Studio/Distributor*: Gramercy; *Running Time*: 99 minutes; *Release Date*: 28 April, 1995, USA; *Rating*: R; *DVD*: *Region 1*: Universal, November 1998, 2.35:1, with weblinks; *Region 2*: NA.

Premise: A heist that goes badly and a threesome that ends badly, told in flashbacks

In adapting Robert Siodmak and Daniel Fuchs' *Criss Cross* (1949), Steven Soderbergh was in retrenching mode, trying, as he said in several interviews, to figure out why he wanted to make movies in the first place. But although *Criss Cross* inspires the film, *Underneath* is also virtually a remake of the director's career-launching *sex lies and videotape*. As in the earlier film, a wayward man returns to disrupt a seemingly settled group of intimates. It's a theme that pops up in all of Soderbergh's apparent 'personal' films. Thus the director either naturally gravitates to material that resonates with his moods, or when it deviates from his interests he bends it to his will. The end of the film is much different from the source, and intersects with the trend in 1990s crime films to titillate the viewer with successive false endings, a trick whose roots are found in teen horror films of the 1970s. *Underneath* also holds the seeds to later Soderbergh films, such as *Traffic*, with its colour-coded sequences.

1996

✸ *Sidney* [*Hard Eight*]; *Director*: Paul Thomas Anderson; *Writer:* Anderson; *Key Cast*: Philip Baker Hall (Sydney), John C. Reilly (John Finnegan). Gwyneth Paltrow (Clementine), Samuel L. Jackson (Jimmy); *Cinematography*: Robert Elswit;

Music: Michael Penn; *Studio/Distributor:* MGM; *Running Time*: 102 minutes; *Release Date*: 20 January 1996, Sundance; *Rating*: R; *DVD*: *Region 1*: Columbia–Tristar, October 1999, 2.35:1, with director commentary, cast commentary, deleted scenes, script lab footage; *Region 2*: NA.

Premise: A Reno gambler takes on a protégé

Hard Eight is in the interesting position of being liked more by the reviewers than its director, who had problems with the distributor. What the critics like is that same quality that informs the later *Sexy Beast*, a plot that, although clear and understandable as you go along, hides jewels of mystery and insight (in this case Sydney's motivation). It should also be noted that Anderson is a brilliant, dependable director of actors and stager of scenes of conflict.

✳ ***Last Man Standing***; *Director:* Walter Hill; *Writer:* Hill, from Kurosawa's *Yojimbo* (and therefore Hammett's *Red Harvest*); *Key Cast*: Bruce Willis (John Smith), Bruce Dern (Sheriff Ed Galt), Christopher Walken (Hickey); *Cinematography*: Lloyd Ahern; *Music*: Ry Cooder; *Studio/Distributor:* New Line; *Running Time*: 101 minutes; *Release Date*: 20 September 1996, USA; *Rating*: R; *DVD*: *Region 1*: New Line, November 1997, 2.35:1; *Region 2*: Entertainment in Video, July 1999, with making of.

Premise: Same as *Yojimbo*, but with a southwest setting

A not entirely successful remake of *Yojimbo* (itself borrowed from Hammett's *Red Harvest*), set in the Prohibition era southwest, Hill's film suffers from the director's perennial bugaboo, casting problems, both at the top and throughout the supporting players. Still, it's an entertaining attempt.

2 Days in the Valley; *Director:* John Herzfeld; *Writer:* Herzfeld; *Key Cast:* Jeff Daniels (Alvin Strayer), Teri Hatcher (Becky Foxx), James Spader (Lee Woods), Eric Stoltz (Wes Taylor); *Cinematography:* Oliver Wood; *Music:* Anthony Marinelli; *Studio/Distributor:* MGM; *Running Time:* 104 minutes; *Release Date:* 12 September 1996, Toronto Film Festival; *Rating:* R; *DVD: Region 1:* HBO, December 1997, 2.35:1 (but non-anamorphic); *Region 2:* NA.

Premise: The high and low lives of several San Fernando valley residents intersect

In the wake of Tarantino's breakthrough films in the early 1990s, numerous competitors came out of the woodwork, either capitalising on the new appetite for 'quirky' dialogue and characters in a crime setting, or finally able to realise otherwise dormant but similar projects. This minor effort is something akin to Quentin Tarantino meeting *Umberto D* (director Paul Mazursky plays a failed writer–director trying to give away his terrier before committing suicide). *2 Days* is also in that cluster of contemporaneous releases that critic Shawn Levy calls "web of life films," in which a collection of disparate people is slowly revealed to be connected. Set in the San Fernando Valley (which Paul Thomas Anderson has imbued with a mythological importance in some of his films) on the hottest day of the year, the tale blends hit men, art collectors, failed Olympic athletes, and undercover cops in a carefully worked out mélange that renders the big valley quite small. To its credit, the film does have numerous clever plot turns. It also features one of the great cinematic catfights.

1997

✱ *U Turn*; *Director*: Oliver Stone; *Writer*: John Ridley; *Key Cast*: Sean Penn (Bobby Cooper), Nick Nolte (Jake McKenna), Jennifer Lopez (Grace McKenna); *Cinematography*: Robert Richardson; *Music*: Ennio Morricone; *Studio/Distributor*: Sony; *Running Time*: 125 minutes; *Release Date*: 27 August 1997, Telluride Film Festival; *Rating*: R; *DVD*: *Region 1*: Columbia–Tristar, March 1997, 1.85:1; *Region 2*: Columbia–Tristar.

Premise: A mysterious traveler is stranded in a Southwest town

With his Native American fixation and addiction to harsh settings, Oliver Stone is a near-natural film soleil director. In fact, in *U Turn* one of the characters even says, "It's the desert that makes you crazy. The loneliness out here. Nobody to talk to. People on the run" – perhaps the clearest summary of 1990s soleil. Unlike the Coens, however, in this instance Stone is unable to balance humor with horror, and the simplistic plot is overwhelmed by a host of eccentric characters. Still, Stone's sympathy with the setting earns back a lot of otherwise dissipated energy.

1998

Montana; *Director*: Jennifer Leitzes; *Writer:* Erich and Jon Hoeber; *Key Cast*: Kyra Sedgwick (Claire Kelsky), Stanley

Tucci (Nicholas Roth); *Cinematography*: Ken Kelsch; *Music*: Cliff Eidelman; *Studio/Distributor*: Columbia-Tristar; *Running Time*: 96 minutes; *Release Date*: 16 January 1998 *(Sundance Film Festival)*; *Rating*: R; *DVD*: *Region 1*: Columbia-Tristar, February 2003, 1.85:1; *Region 2*: NA.

Premise: The travails of a hit woman

Montana is one of those movies that seems like every other film of its kind that you've seen lately. However, it has distinguishing characteristics. Made by first time director Leitzes it aspires to Tarantino-level coolness about violence, but as it is directed by a woman, it strives to portray a dubious equality of womanhood among criminals. Claire (Sedgwick) is the loyal enforcer for her beloved boss, called The Boss (Robbie Coltrane, in what you could call a "one room performance"). Her partner is Nick (Tucci), who secretly loves her, and whom she secretly loves. Kitty (Robin Tunney) is the boss' troublesome girlfriend. Complications ensue. After (not enough) gun fights few of these people are left alive. *Montana* has many of the earmarks of the indie film. Most of it is set in one place. There is a conglomeration of cast members whom you wouldn't normally link up with each other. There is also the inclusion of a TV has-been (John Ritter) looking for a comeback to add 'ironic' wit. And there is a lot of talk. Talk is cheap and people talk and talk and talk in this movie without saying anything, or worse, saying anything witty. There's something static about all these quasi-indie films that want to be Hollywood movies when they grow up.

1999

✳ *The Limey*; *Director*: Steven Soderbergh; *Writer*: Lem Dobbs; *Key Cast*: Terence Stamp (Wilson), Lesley Ann Warren (Elaine), Luis Guzman (Eduardo Roel), Peter Fonda (Terry Valentine); *Cinematography*: Ed Lachman; *Music*: Cliff Martinez; *Studio/Distributor*: Artisan; *Running Time*: 89 minutes; *Release Date*: 15 May 1999, Cannes Film Festival; *Rating*: R; *DVD*: *Region 1*: Artisan, March 2000, 1.85:1, with director–writer commentary, actor commentary, isolated musical score, making of; *Region 2*: Highlight, September 2000, with interviews and B-Roll.

Premise: A British gangster visits Los Angeles in order to investigate the death of his daughter

A self-conscious evocation of 1960s crime films *Poor Cow* and *Get Carter*, most explicitly, Soderbergh and Dobbs's film also evokes Boorman from *Point Blank* and other New Wave inflected visual tricks culled from Resnais and others. Although some of its tricks are meant to thwart audience expectations (such as withholding a brawl from the viewer's eyes) it's a deeply satisfying thriller on many levels, cinematically and culturally.

✳ *The Woman Chaser*; *Director*: Robinson Devor; *Writer*: Devor from the Charles Willeford novel; *Key Cast*: Patrick Warburton (Richard Hudson), Eugene Roche (Used Car Dealer), Emily Newman (Laura); *Cinematography*: Kramer Morgenthau; *Music*: Daniele Luppi; *Studio/Distributor*: Asylum; *Running Time*: 90 minutes; *Release Date*: 8 October 1999 *(New York Film Festival)*; *Rating*: R; *DVD*: NA.

Premise: A used car salesman tries to get his film made

Probably the most underrated movie of its year, this comical enterprise is not only one of the best movies about movie making, it is one of the film films to either attempt and succeed at capturing the wit at the heart of novelist Charles Willeford's anarchic spirit. Warburton's driven, opaque protagonist is an unexpected treasure.

Additional, Potential, or Honorary Films Soleils: 1990: *Bad Influence, The Two Jakes, Boiling Point* (Kitano), *Miller's Crossing, Q&A, Desperate Hours*; 1991: *Blue Desert, Cape Fear, Barton Fink, Mortal Thoughts*; 1992: *Storyville, Basic Instinct, Unlawful Entry, Past Midnight*; 1993: *Suture, Romeo is Bleeding, True Romance, Boiling Point* (Harris); 1994: *The Last Seduction, Pulp Fiction, Natural Born Killers, Chunking Express*; 1995: *Things to Do in Denver When You're Dead, Casino, Get Shorty, The Usual Suspects, Heat, se7en*; 1996: *Fargo, Heaven's Prisoners, Blood and Wine, Bound*; 1997: *City of Industry, Donnie Brasco, Cop Land, Lost Highway, This World, Then The Fireworks*; 1998: *Clay Pigeons, Thick as Thieves, The Big Lebowski, Wild Things, Out of Sight, A Simple Plan, Following*; 1999: *8mm, Humanité, Fight Club, Simpatico, Double Jeopardy*.

The 21st Century

As the first decade of cinema's second century reaches the mid-way mark, it turns out that Cinema is in a barely acknowledged state of crisis. Ticket sales are down, partially because most films are crap, and partially because of improved competition from television, games, DVDs, web surfing, and other media. It seems as if, internationally speaking, more movies than ever are made, yet the media only promote one or two at a time and small gems get lost. And the state of the world is so tense that mere movie watching seems frivolous. The mass public seems both more isolated and more volatile than ever before. Film soleil continues to be a good vehicle for exploring these tensions.

2000

Under Suspicion; *Director:* Stephen Hopkins; *Writer:* Tom Provost and W. Peter Iliff, from the Claude Miller movie, *Garde à vue*; *Key Cast:* Gene Hackman (Henry Hearst), Morgan Freeman (Captain Victor Benezet), Thomas Jane (Detective Felix Owens), Monica Bellucci (Chantal Hearst); *Cinematography:* Peter Levy; *Music:* Numerous artists; *Studio/Distributor:* Lion's Gate; *Running Time:* 110 minutes; *Release Date:* 11 May 2000 Cannes Film Festival; *Rating:* R; *DVD: Region 1:* Columbia–Tristar, January 2001, 1.85:1, with director and actor commentary, making of; *Region 2:* Splendid, December 2001, with video interviews, making ofs.

Premise: Two cops interrogate a prominent citizen

One of most interesting minor genres doesn't have an official name but consists of a story built around an interrogation. It proves to be a surprisingly cinematic premise. A subset of the *policier*, such films are most often existential studies in psychology, identity and will. Interrogation films include *A Pure Formality*, *Mortal Thoughts* and *Closet Land*. Other films more loosely strung on interrogations include *Detective Story*, *The Usual Suspects*, *Rashomon*, *Following*, *One Hour Photo*,

Identity, *The Prisoner* (1955), *Przesluchanie* (Richard Bugajski, 1982), *The Interview* (Craig Monahan, 1998), *The Offence* (1973), and *Killing Me Softly*. The TV series *Homicide: Life on the Streets* frequently employed the interrogation as a dominating device. *Under Suspicion* is only the most recent film to focus intensely on an interrogation, and it in turn was based on Claude Miller's 1981 film, itself based on John Wainwright's novel *Brainwash*. Set in Puerto Rico (for no particular narrative reason), this entry in the interrogation sweeps 'opens up' the story to flashbacks, recreations, and scenes set outside the room of inquiry, even though the story occurs over the course of four hours. The film is surprisingly good without being ambitious. While San Juan celebrates the Festival of San Sebastian, and during a fundraiser for hurricane disaster-relief, prominent tax lawyer Henry Hearst (Hackman) is questioned in the police station across the street by his long-time acquaintance Victor Benezet (Freeman). Despite his reputation, Hearst is suspected of killing two girls on the island; ultimately his role in the case has more to do with his strained relationship with his glamorous wife (Monica Bellucci). Hopkins and credited writers Thomas Provost and W. Peter Iliff create an interesting contrast between Hearst and Victor, both in their private and professional lives, and Hopkins employs a fluid and rather fascinating editing style that shows the influence of both Nicolas Roeg and Oliver Stone, which keeps the film visually interesting. Quietly intense performances come from the noteworthy cast as well, and Thomas Jane, as Victor's impetuous associate, echoes the relationship between the Freeman and Brad Pitt characters in *Se7en*.

❊ *Memento*; *Director*: Christopher Nolan; *Writer*: Nolan, from a story by Jonathan Nolan; *Key Cast*: Guy Pearce

(Leonard Shelby), Carrie-Anne Moss (Natalie), Joe Pantoliano (Teddy Gammell); *Cinematography*: Wally Pfister; *Music*: David Julyan; *Studio/Distributor:* Newmarket; *Running Time*: 113 minutes; *Release Date*: 5 September 2000, Venice Film Festival; *Rating*: R; *DVD*: *Region 1*: Columbia-Tristar, September, 2001 and then May, 2002, 2.35:1, the first disc with audio commentary, the second with making ofs, anatomy of a scene, stills, sketches, original script, original short story, trailers, both with confusing menus; *Region 2*: Columbia-Tristar, July 2002, with director commentary, interview, making of, stills, screenplay.

Premise: A man, suffering from short-term memory loss, uses notes and tattoos to record clues revealing his wife's killer

Memento delights because it taxes the brain as it unveils its mystery from two directions at once. Leonard Shelby is a driven insurance investigator looking for the man who killed his wife. In counterpoint to that forward direction, the narrative covers his actions backwards, each slightly overlapping scene tugging the viewer back one step. But Shelby is the opposite of a Jim Thompson hero, a person whom everyone underestimates. Here, everyone uses Shelby, because he suffers from short-term memory loss. Thus he is victim first to a rogue vice cop who sets him on his drug-dealing opponents, and then the tool for revenge by the film's femme fatale. Both the cop and the femme fatale use Shelby's short spells of consciousness to their advantage at crucial moments. *Memento* asks intriguing questions, because there are also hints that Shelby's syndrome is hysterical in origin. "And memories can be distorted," he says. "They're just an interpretation, they're not a record, and they're irrelevant if you have the facts." What's tragically paradoxical is that at almost every point Shelby does have the facts. But because of his "syndrome" he is blinded to them.

✻ *Way of the Gun*; *Director*: Christopher McQuarrie; *Writer*: McQuarrie; *Key Cast*: James Caan (Joe Sarno), Benicio Del Toro (Longbaugh), Juliette Lewis (Robin), Ryan Phillippe (Parker); *Cinematography*: Dick Pope; *Music*: Joe Kraemer; *Studio/Distributor*: Artisan; *Running Time*: 119 minutes; *Release Date*: 8 September 2000, USA; *Rating*: R; *DVD*: Region 1: Artisan, January 2001, 1.85:1, with director commentary, isolated music score with composer commentary, interviews, B-Roll, deleted scene; *Region 2*: NA.

Premise: Two drifters kidnap a pregnant girl

"There's always free cheese in a mousetrap," says Del Toro's Longbaugh (named after the Sundance Kid) near the end of this masterly, brilliant, hilarious, and entertaining film. Sadly, *Way of the Gun* received little pre-release hype (unusual these days), then played little more than a week before vanishing into the video stores. Yet *Way of the Gun* will loom large in the history of film soleil, perhaps as the genre's last truly great film thanks to the fact that it is visually stylish, iconically acted, narratively clever, and has great, quotable dialogue. The "mousetrap" is of Longbaugh and his partner Parker's own devising, and although through most of the film they are quite clever when faced with the unexpected, ultimately they end where they begin: in the dirt. *Way of the Gun* is about quiet competence and Hemingwayesque grace under pressure. Longbaugh and Parker communicate with each other almost wordlessly. It's an ultra-violent, foul-mouthed, stylish film, but as director and writer Christopher McQuarrie (who won an Oscar for writing *The Usual Suspects*) was at pains to explain in the November 2001 *Sight and Sound*, this action thriller is actually a refutation of the easy violence and empty posing of Tarantino and his disciples. Instead of in Tarantino's films, *Way*'s roots lie in Sam Peckinpah, who liked nothing more than to rip the guts out of a guy with bullets under the hot sun, while lamenting how standards in criminal conduct and violence were falling everywhere. As Benicio Del Toro laments, today's violent poseurs "want to be criminals more then they want to commit crime."

❋ *Sexy Beast*; *Director:* Jonathan Glazer; *Writer:* Louis Mellis, David Scinto, and Andrew Michael Jolley; *Key Cast*: Ray Winstone (Gary 'Gal' Dove), Ben Kingsley (Don Logan), Ian McShane (Teddy Bass); *Cinematography*: Ivan Bird and Dan Landin; *Music*: Roque Baños; *Studio/Distributor*: FilmFour; *Running Time*: 89 minutes; *Release Date*: 13 September 2000, *Toronto Film Festival*; *Rating*: R; *DVD*: *Region 1*: Fox, March 2002, 1.85:1, with actor-producer commentary, making of.; *Region 2*: Fox, March 2002, 2.35:1, with making of, interviews, deleted scenes, B-Roll, posters.

Premise: A retired gangster is pulled back in for one more job

There are a few mysteries at the heart of Glazer's excellent, wryly funny, and visually lively British gangster film. The film's set up is that the frightening Don Logan (a smoldering Kingsley) has come to Spain to fetch back the retired Gal Dove (Winstone) for another job, on behalf of McShane's gangster. But in retrospect, it seems like quite a bit of a detour for Logan to go all the way to Spain to get a guy whom all agree isn't quite right for the job. Although it is never explicitly stated, Logan has a hidden agenda, which is to see Jackie (Julianne White), the girlfriend of Gal's co-retiree. Logan had some sort of no-doubt brutal and uninvited sex with her a few years earlier and he found that he "quite liked her." That's Gal's bad luck. Another puzzle concerns No. 1 gangster McShane and his activities. Ultimately, *Sexy Beast* has the affect of a low intensity *Memento*, with a story you piece together after the fact, and it's all the better for it.

✻ *Traffic*; *Director:* Steven Soderbergh; *Writer:* Steve Gaghan, from the British miniseries *Traffick*; *Key Cast:* Benicio Del Toro (Javier Rodriguez), Michael Douglas (Robert Wakefield), Don Cheadle (Montel Gordon); *Cinematography:* Soderbergh; *Music:* Cliff Martinez; *Studio/Distributor:* USA Films; *Running Time:* 147 minutes; *Release Date:* 27 December 2000, USA; *Rating:* R; *DVD:* *Region 1:* USA, May 2001, 1.85:1, with making of, stills; also, Criterion Collection, May 2002, with director-writer commentary, producer commentary, composer commentary, deleted scenes, numerous making ofs; *Region 2:* Entertainment in Video, July 2001, with deleted scenes, B-Roll.

Premise: The international drug trade dramatised, following the traffickers and the trafficking routes into the US

In one of the most telling lines in this sweeping look at the international drug trade, a trafficker turned snitch (Miguel Ferrer) point blank tells his arresting-officer-turned-handler (Don Cheadle) that, thanks to machinations south of the border by a competing drug cartel seeking to put Ferrer's boss out of business, Cheadle's character now works for a drug dealer too. It's probably the sharpest observation in a film that alternates such insights with much more conventional anti-drug propaganda. Based on the British mini-series but transplanted to Mexico, Cincinnati, and San Diego, Gaghan's script weaves three complex, interconnecting tales to portray drug trafficking's dire effect on society. Soderbergh's hand-held, New Wave approach to his colour-coded sequences enforces verisimilitude when the text itself lapses into middlebrow lectures on the hazards of drugs. It's probably an object lesson to filmmakers in how to make a social protest film that cleverly illustrates its points cinematically when you don't really care about the subject all that much in the first place. The storyline featuring Benicio Del Toro is the most powerful, human, and moving, and there is something magical about the film's concluding scene, with its display of his quiet triumph, accompanied by Cliff Martinez's exotic score.

2001

✳ *The Man Who Wasn't There* [*The Barber*]; *Director:* Joel Coen; *Writer:* The Coens; *Key Cast:* Billy Bob Thornton (Ed Crane), Frances McDormand (Doris Crane), Michael Badalucco (Frank), James Gandolfini (Dave Brewster); *Cinematography:* Roger Deakins; *Music:* Carter Burwell; *Studio/Distributor:* Gramercy; *Running Time:* 116 minutes; *Release Date:* 13 May 2001, Cannes Film Festival; *Rating:* R; *DVD: Region 1:* USA, April 2002, 1.85:1, with star and director commentary, making of, DP interview, deleted scenes, stills; *Region 2:* BMG Video, May, 2002, with B-Roll, cast and crew credits.

Premise: A barber suspects his wife of cheating on him

The Coens can't resist making a joke. In the chamber piece hothouse of this black and white evocation of noirs past, probably influenced by Cornell Woolrich this time as the brothers methodically adapt, unofficially anyway, all the great American mystery writers of the 20th Century, they alternate broad humor with the dark story of a vengeful husband. The mix didn't work for a lot of reviewers and so yet again a Coen Brothers movie was met with cultural indifference and low box office. Coen-heads meanwhile shake their heads in dismay at the fact that the most consistently brilliant string of movies in the history of the medium has not received its due. The Coen Brothers do it right. Their films are cleverly, solidly written, they are well cast, beautifully shot, and exquisitely scored. Their films reward repeat viewings and quiet contemplation. More books have been written about the Coen Brothers than any other working filmmakers. Yet for some reason the public disdains them, like Baudelaire's dog in *Paris Spleen*, who prefers the smell of excrement to a bottle of perfume. "In this you resemble the public, which should never be offered delicate perfumes that infuriate them, but only carefully selected garbage."

Who is Cletis Tout?; *Director*: Chris Ver Wiel; *Writer:* Ver Wiel; *Key Cast*: Christian Slater (Trevor Allen Finch), Portia de Rossi (Tess Donnelly); *Cinematography*: Jerzy Zielinski; *Music*: Randy Edelman, Jeremy Sweet; *Studio/Distributor*: Paramount; *Running Time*: 92 minutes; *Release Date*: 12 September 2001, Toronto Film Festival; *Rating*: R; *DVD*: *Region 1*: Paramount, Jan 2003, 2.35:1; *Region 2*: NA.

Premise: An escaped con's adoption of a new identity leads to trouble

Who is Cletis Tout is a movie with 16 credited producers, yet not one of whom could manage to get the film released to cinemas. Perhaps that's because it was perceived that audiences were finally fed up with Tarantino inspired imitators such as *8 Heads in a Duffel Bag* and *2 Days in the Valley,* Tarantino's movies still exert a remarkable appeal born of their intensity and visual flair. Of course, few of his imitators adopt these traits. Instead, what they mimic are his pop culture references and reverence for the cult of the killer. *Cletis* has lots of shoulder shrugging hoods out of the *Sopranos* talking about the gay ironies of *Deliverance.* There was a time when a young filmmaker made a cheap exploitation horror film in order to get a foot in the door of Hollywood. Now, they make cheap exploitation crime films. *Cletis,* however, ends up not having the courage of its convicts. The film is Tarantino lite; a softer, gentler Tarantino for a new generation. That's because, as with many crime films, it's really a love story. That's not Tarantino's fault either. One can't blame a god for the actions of his worst acolytes, who turn his reservoir dogs into pulp.

Knockaround Guys; *Director:* Brian Koppelman and David Levien; *Writer:* Koppelman and Levien; *Key Cast:* Barry Pepper (Matty Demaret), Vin Diesel (Taylor Reese), John Malkovich (Teddy Deserve); *Cinematography:* Tom Richmond; *Music:* Clint Mansell; *Studio/Distributor:* New Line; *Running Time:* 91 minutes; *Release Date:* 30 November 2001, Italy (October 2002 in the USA); *Rating:* R; *DVD:* *Region 1*: New Line, February 2003, 1.85:1, with director commentary, deleted scenes; *Region 2*: Warner, March 2003, with commentary, deleted scenes.

Premise: Aspiring hoods go to a Montana town to fetch some cash

Before they made Tarantino knock-offs, young filmmakers made knock-offs of Scorsese's films, especially *Mean Streets* with its attractive clutch of chummy aspiring wiseguys who circulate in a female-excluding world where violence breaks out like paradisial rainstorms. Koppelman and Levien's film is the latest in a long line of vaguely *Mean Streets* influenced buddy crime films that includes *Laws of Gravity* (Gomez, 1992), *Federal Hill* (Corrente, 1994), and *Amongst Friends* (Weiss, 1993). In fact, their previous work, the script for *Rounders*, recreates the same good boy-bad boy friendship dynamic found in *Mean Streets*. Barry Pepper's Matty Demaret and his crew end up in Wibaux, Montana to help a money courier get out of a jam. *Knockaround Guys* features a remarkable scene of a bar fight ("500 fights, that's the number I figured when I was a kid. 500 street fights and you could consider yourself a legitimate tough guy") in which Vin Diesel's Reese beats up the local tough guy solely as a beacon signal, emitted to the town as a whole that the guys want their money back. Unfortunately, the rest of the movie percolates at a rather low temperature. Until the inevitable showdowns, reversals and revelations, the film crawls at a stately pace, and the final *Red Rock West* style face-off doesn't feel all that much different from the thousand on the screen before it. Much of the cause of the film's low heat goes to the somber manner in which most of the cast members play their parts. They all seem to be bothered by some tiny, quiet dissatisfaction that saps the energy out of their face and the limberness out of their limbs. This hangdog tribe has none of the pizzazz of Scorsese's mean street denizens.

2002

✻ *The Salton Sea*; *Director:* D.J. Caruso; *Writer:* Tony Gayton; *Key Cast:* Val Kilmer (Danny Parker/Tom Van Allen), Vincent D'Onofrio (Pooh-Bear); *Cinematography*: Amir M. Mokri; *Music:* Thomas Newman; *Studio/Distributor:* Warner; *Running Time*: 103 minutes; *Release Date*: 12 February 2002, Canada; *Rating*: R; *DVD*: *Region 1:* Warner, September 2002, 1.85:1, with making ofs, filmographies, trailer; *Region 2:* Warner, May 2003, with making ofs.

Premise: Adventures in the life of a meth addict and dealer

The Salton Sea is a real place, although not really a sea, and is also the 'Chinatown' of the film, the literal and symbolic locus for a failure of action. *The Salton Sea* starts out being the story of Danny Parker (a brilliant Val Kilmer). He's a heavily tattooed musician turned meth addict who lives in a permanent all-night party of tweaked crazies in a Los Angeles apartment. The film begins with a *Casino*-style history of meth, and then shows Danny and his buddy Jimmy the Finn (an endearing Peter Sarsgaard) going out to refuel the depleted "gak" supplies. But *The Salton Sea* is better seen when thinking that it is just another portrayal of depressing drug addicts. Like the equally ignored master-piece *Heat*, this film has a fantastic cast: Vincent D'Onofrio, Adam Goldberg, Doug Hutchison, Anthony LaPaglia, Deborah Kara Unger, B. D. Wong, R. Lee Ermey and Shalom

Harlow. If nothing else, *The Salton Sea* has the distinction of featuring both of those old standbys, Luis Guzman and Danny Trejo.

2003

Confidence; *Director:* James Foley; *Writer:* Doug Jung; *Key Cast*: Edward Burns (Jake Vig), Rachel Weisz (Lily), Paul Giamatti (Gordo); *Cinematography*: Juan Ruiz Anchía; *Music*: Christophe Beck; *Studio/Distributor:* Lion's Gate; *Running Time*: 97 minutes; *Release Date*: 20 January 2003 Sundance Film Festival; *Rating*: R; *DVD*: *Region 1*: Lion's Gate, September 2003, 1.85:1, with director commentary, cast commentary, writer commentary, anatomy of a scene, deleted scenes; *Region 2*: NA.

Premise: A scam artist is tugged in several directions

James Foley's film shows film soleil alive and well – just compromised by the film industry's obsession with happy endings. *Confidence* concerns a crew of roving con artists who, as the film begins, are winding up a scam. The team consists of Jake Vig (Burns), the ostensive leader, Big Al (Louis Lombardi), Gordo (Paul Giamatti), and Miles (Brian Van Holt). Unfortunately, their mark is a mere agent for someone else called The King (Dustin Hoffman), and through a complicated set of obligations, Vig and his team must work with The King on a specific scam to square things. Although the viewer knows going in that not everyone or everything presented will really be what they seem, what's hidden from the viewer are some of the characters' motivations. These are subtly and cleverly woven into the film's fabric. *Confidence* is reasonably entertaining up until its end. Although the ending is an organic outgrowth of the incidents set up in the movie, it feels too much in line with the sort of 'mega happy' ending that film studios favor these days. The R1 DVD's abundant supplements are notable for the fact that film soleil is actually mentioned.

2005

Assault on Precinct 13; *Director*: Jean-François Richet; *Writer*: James DeMonaco, from John Carpenter's 1976 movie; *Key Cast*: Ethan Hawke (Sgt. Jake Roenick), Laurence Fishburne (Marion Bishop), Maria Bello (Alex Sabian); *Cinematography*: Robert Gantz; *Music*: Graeme Revell; *Studio/Distributor*: Universal; *Running Time*: 109 minutes; *Release Date*: 19 January 2005, USA; *Rating*: R; *DVD*: *Region 1*: Rogue Pictures, May 2005, 2.40:1, with director commentary, making ofs, deleted scenes; *Region 2*: Focus Features/ Entertainment in Video, June 2005, three making ofs and deleted scenes.

Premise: Similar to the Carpenter film, though the motivation is different

Assault may be an unlikely concluding film for a survey of film soleil, i.e., thrillers made in the daylight, given that this remake takes place in Detroit at night over New Year's Eve. But one wants to end a book on a positive note, and the alternative was *Be Cool*. Still, *Assault* as a remake charts subtle differences between the American soleil cinema of the 1970s, when Carpenter's film was released, and the present, some 200 film soleil later. The most striking shift is that the cops are now the villains. It's a given. It's understood. If Carpenter's film was about the randomness of violence, like so many of contemporary films (*The Incident, Little Murders, The Taking of Pelham One Two Three*), reflecting a terrified citizenry concerned about the destruction of their cozy life, the new one is a psychological essay on guilt, on our collective 'inwardness' in the Cyber 'Oughts. Also, making the cops the bad guys shifts the film into a political spectrum, one anathema to Carpenter himself. With the cops made the baddies, the film calls into question the drug war, the authenticity of the assigned roles of cops and robbers, and the rush to judgment we make of the criminal classes, humanised in the film by John Lequizamo and others. Also, the cops and crooks under siege have more motivation to stick together in this moment of urgency, creating more tensions. With its more complex backstory and visual pyrotechnics, the new *Assault* ends up in many ways better than its progenitor.

Additional, Potential, or Honorary Films Soleils: 2000: *Suzhou River, Brother, Diamond Men*; 2001: *Mulholland Dr., The Pledge, The Deep End, The Mexican, The Hard Word, Made, Lantana, Training Day*; 2002: *The Good Thief, Dark Blue, Ripley's Game, Narc, Insomnia, demonlover, Minority Report*; 2003: *Basic, The Cooler, Holes, City of God, Out of Time*; 2004: *Suspect Zero, Collateral, The Ladykillers*; 2005: *Be Cool.*

4. Reference Materials
Books about Film Noir

A Girl and a Gun: The Complete Guide To Film Noir On Video, David N. Meyer, Avon, 1997, Trade Paperback, 303 pages, ISBN 0 380 79067 X.

A Reference Guide to the American Film: 1940 – 1958 Noir, Robert Ottoson, The Scarecrow Press, 1981, Hardback, 285 pages, ISBN 0 8108 1363 7.

The Art of Noir: The Posters and Graphics from the Classic Era of Noir, Eddie Muller, The Overlook Press, 2002, Hardback, 271 pages, ISBN 1 58567 073 1.

Autopsy: An Element of Realism in Film Noir, Carl Richardson, The Scarecrow Press, 1992, Hardback, 247 pages, ISBN 0 8108 2496 5.

Bad: Infamy, Darkness, Evil and Slime on Screen, Murray Pomerance, editor, State University of New York Press, 2004, Trade Paperback, 357 pages, ISBN 0 7914 5940 3.

Black and White and Noir: America's Pulp Modernism, Paula Rabinowitz, Columbia University Press, 2002, Trade Paperback, 308 pages, ISBN 0 231 11481 8.

British Crime Cinema, Steve Chibnall and Robert Murphy, editors, Routledge, 1999, Trade Paperback, 251 pages, ISBN 0 415 16870 8.

Crime Films, Thomas Leitch, Cambridge University Press, 2002, Trade Paperback, 282 pages, ISBN 0 521 64671 5.

Crime Movie Posters, Bruce Hershenson, Hershenson–Allen Archive, 1997, Trade Paperback, unpaginated, ISBN 1 887893 19 9.

Crime Movies: An Illustrated History, Carlos Clarens, Norton, 1980, Trade Paperback, 351 pages, ISBN 0 393 01262 X.

Crime Scenes: Movie Poster Art of the Film Noir, Lawrence Bassoff, Lawrence Bassoff Collection, Inc., 1997, Trade Paperback, 159 pages, ISBN 1 886310 11 4.

Dark City: The Film Noir, Spencer Selby, McFarland, 1983, Hardback, 255 pages, ISBN 0 89950 103 6.

Dark City: The Lost World of Film Noir, Eddie Muller, St. Martin's Griffin, 1998, Trade Paperback, 206 pages, ISBN 0 312 18076 4.

Death on the Cheap: The Lost B-Movies of Film Noir, Arthur Lyons, Da Capo, 2000, Trade Paperback, 212 pages, ISBN 0 306 80996 6.

Detours and Lost Highways: A Map of Neo-Noir, Foster Hirsch, Limelight Editions, 1999, Trade Paperback, 398 pages, ISBN 0 87910 288 8.

Dreams and Dead Ends: The American Gangster Film, Jack Shadoian, MIT, 1977, Hardback, 366 pages, ISBN 0 262 19159 8.

Dreams and Dead Ends: The American Gangster Film, Second Edition, Jack Shadoian, Oxford University Press, 2003, Trade Paperback, 376 pages, ISBN 0 19 514292 6.

Film Noir: Films of Trust and Betrayal, Paul Duncan, Pocket Essentials, 2000, Trade Paperback, 96 pages, ISBN 1 903047 08 0.

Early Film Noir: Greed, Lust, and Murder Hollywood Style, William Hare, McFarland, 2003, Trade Paperback, 211 pages, ISBN 0 7864 1629 7.

The Erotic Thriller In Contemporary Cinema, Linda Ruth

Williams, Indiana University Press, 2005, Trade paperback, 466 pp, ISBN 0 253 34713 0.

Film Noir, Alain Silver and James Ursini, Taschen, 2004, Trade Paperback, 191 pages, ISBN 3 8228 2261 2.

Film Noir, Andrew Spicer, Longman, 2002, Trade Paperback, 250 pages, ISBN 0 582 43712 1.

Film Noir: A Comprehensive Illustrated Reference, Michael L. Stephens, McFarland, 1994, Hardback, 424 pages, ISBN 0 89950 802 2.

Film Noir and the Spaces of Modernity, Edward Dimendberg, Harvard University Press, 2004, Trade Paperback, 327 pages, ISBN 0 674 01314 X.

Film Noir: An Encyclopedic Reference to the American Style, Third Edition, Alain Silver and Elizabeth Ward, editors, The Overlook Press, 1992, Trade Paperback, 479 pages, ISBN 0 87951 479 5.

Film Noir Guide: 745 Films of the Classic Era, 1940-1959, Michael F. Keaney, McFarland, 2003, Hardback, 541 pages, ISBN 0 786 41547 9.

Film Noir: Reflections in a Dark Mirror, Bruce Crowther, Columbus Books, 1988, Trade Paperback, 192 pages, ISBN 0 86287 402 5.

Film Noir Reader, Alain Silver and James Ursini, editors, Limelight Editions, 1996, Trade Paperback, 343 pages, ISBN 0 87910 197 0.

Film Noir Reader 2, Alain Silver and James Ursini, editors, Limelight Editions, 1999, Trade Paperback, 346 pages, ISBN 0 87910 280 2.

Film Noir Reader 3, Robert Porfirio, Alain Silver, and James Ursini, editors, Limelight Editions, 2002, Trade Paperback, 239 pages, ISBN 0 87910 961 0.

Film Noir Reader 4: The Crucial Films and Themes, Alain Silver and James Ursini, editors, Limelight Editions, 2004, Trade Paperback, 326 pages, ISBN 0 87910 305 1.

French Film Noir, Robin Buss, Marion Boyers, 1993, Hardback, 224 pages, ISBN 0 7145 2963 X.

The Great Gangster Pictures, James Robert Parish and Michael R. Pitts, The Scarecrow Press, 1976, Hardback, 431 pages, ISBN 0 8108 0881 1.

Hard-Boiled: Great Lines from Classic Noir Films, Peggy Thompson and Saeko Usukawa, Chronicle Books, 1995, Trade Paperback, 124 pages, ISBN 0 289 80151 6.

Hollywood's Dark Cinema: The American Film Noir, R. Barton Palmer, Twayne Publishers, 1993, Trade Paperback, 206 pages, ISBN 0 8057 9335 6.

In a Lonely Street: Film Noir, Genre, Masculinity, Frank Krutnik, Routledge, 1991, Trade Paperback, 268 pages, ISBN 0 415 02630 X.

Le Film Noir, Patrick Brion, Nathan Image, 1991, Hardback, 361 pages, ISBN 2 09 240017 7.

Mean Streets and Raging Bill: The Legacy of Film Noir in Contemporary American Cinema, Richard Martin, Scarecrow, 1999, Trade Paperback, 199 pages, ISBN 0 8108 3642 4.

More than Night: Film Noir in Contexts, James Naremore, University of California Press, 1997, Trade Paperback, 345 pages, ISBN 0 520 21294 0.

The Movie Book of Film Noir, Ian Cameron, editor, Studio Vista, 1992, Hardback, 288 pages, ISBN 0 289 80048 X.

Mystery, Violence, and Popular Culture, John G. Calwelti, Popular Press/University of Wisconsin Press, 2005, Trade Paperback, 410 pages, ISBN 0 299 19634 8.

Neo-Noir: The New Film Noir Style, Ronald Schwartz, Scarecrow, 2005, Trade Paperback, 160 pages, ISBN 0 810 85676 X.

Noir Anxiety, Kelly Oliver and Benigno Trigo, University of Minnesota Press, 2002, Trade Paperback, 297 pages, ISBN 0 8166 4110 2.

Noir Fiction: Dark Highways, Paul Duncan, Pocket Essentials, 2003, Trade Paperback, 96 pages, ISBN 1 903047 11 0.

The Noir Style, Alain Silver and James Ursini, The Overlook Press, 1999, Hardback, 248 pages, ISBN 0 87951 722 0.

Out of the Past: Adventures In Film Noir, Barry Gifford, University Press of Mississippi, 2000, Trade Paperback, 190 pages, ISBN 0 275 95332 7.

A Panorama of American Film Noir 1941 – 1953, Raymond Borde and Etienne Chaumeton, City Lights Books, 1955, 2002, Trade Paperback, 242 pages, ISBN 0 87286 412 X.

Pump 'Em Full of Lead: A Look at Gangsters on Film, Marilyn Yaquinto, Twayne, 1998, Trade Paperback, 265 pages, ISBN 0 8057 3892 4.

Queen of the 'B's: Ida Lupino Behind the Camera, Annette Kuhn, editor, Praeger, 1995, Trade Paperback, 202 pages, ISBN 0 306 80996 6.

Shades of Noir, Joan Copjec, Verso, 1997, Trade Paperback, 300 pages, ISBN 0 86091 625 1.

Somewhere in the Night: Film Noir and the American City, Nicholas Christopher, Free Press, 1997, Hardback, 290 pages, ISBN 0 684 82803 0.

Spies and Sleuths, James J. Mulay, CineBooks, 1988, Trade Paperback, 211 pages, ISBN 0 684 82803 0.

Street With No Name: A History of the Classic American Film Noir, Andrew Dickos, University Press of Kentucky, 2002, Hardback, 307 pages, ISBN 0 8131 2243 0.

Underworld, U.S.A., Colin McArthur, Secker and Warburg, 1972, Trade Paperback, 176 pages, ISBN 436 09885 7.

Voices in the Dark: The Narrative Patterns of Film Noir, J. P.

Telotte, University of Illinois Press, 1988, Trade Paperback, 248 pages, ISBN 0 252 06056 3.

Women in Film Noir, E. Ann Kaplan, BFI Publishing, 1978, 1980, Hardback, 132 pages, ISBN 0 85170 105 1.

Women in Film Noir: New Edition, E. Ann Kaplan, BFI Publishing, 1998, Trade Paperback, 238 pages, ISBN 0 85170 666 5.

Noir on the Web

Disappointingly, there are no fully satisfying, thorough, and detailed websites dedicated to film noir and related subjects. Here are a few that are at least informative.

Film Noir, an introduction and survey of the subject: http://www.filmsite.org/filmnoir.html

Classic Noir OnLine, a links page to the IMDB: http://www.classicnoir.com/

Other References

The American Cinema: Directors and Directions, 1929 – 1968, Andrew Sarris, Dutton, 1968, Hardback, 383 pages.

Arthur Penn, Robin Wood, Praeger, 1970, Hardback, 144 pages.

Bad Girls: Film Fatales, Sirens, and Molls, Tony Turtu, Collectors Press, 2005, Hardback, 176 pages, ISBN 1 933112 03 4.

A Field Guide to American Houses, Virginia and Lee McAlester, Knopf, 1984, Trade Paperback, 525 pages, ISBN 0 394 73969 8.

Figures Traced in Light: On Cinematic Staging, David Bordwell, University of California Press, 2005, Trade Paperback, 314 pages, ISBN 0 520 24197 5

The Gangster Film, Phil Hardy, editors, Overlook, 1998, Hardback, 512 pages, ISBN 087951 881 2.

Jean Renoir, Raymond Durgnat, University of California Press, 1974, Hardback, 429 pages, ISBN 0 520 02283

Kings of the Bs, Todd McCarthy and Charles Flynn, editors, Dutton, 1975, Hardback, 561 pages, ISBN 0 525 14090 5.

Running Away from Myself, Barbara Deming, Grossman, 1969, Hardback, 210 pages, ISBN 0 525 14090 5.

The Essential Library: Literature Best-Sellers

Build up your library with new titles published every month

Alan Moore by Lance Parkin

"Alan Moore Knows the Score," as Pop Will Eat Itself sang. For over 20 years, from early work on British weekly comics *2000AD* and *Warrior* to today, as the writer of *From Hell* and the America's Best Comics line, Moore has stretched the boundaries of the comics medium. Moore is prolific and his work crosses genre boundaries like few others, ranging from farce and high comedy to the dark, grim work that epitomised the comics revolution of the late 1980s. This book examines recurring themes and how Moore's work has evolved over the years.

Joel & Ethan Coen by Colin Odell & Michelle LeBlanc

Intelligent, experimental, frightening, funny and always delightfully surprising, Coen brothers' films mark a constant high-point in the cinema of the Eighties and Nineties. Their eccentric vision is born of a unique relationship: Joel Coen directs, Ethan produces, they both write. Although their films share many themes and, indeed, many actors, their subjects range from the hard noir of *Blood Simple* via the sophisticated fantasy of *The Hudsucker Proxy* to the frostbitten comedy-of-errors of *Fargo*.

As well as an introductory essay, each of the Coen brothers' films is discussed in detail, including the enigmatic *Miller's Crossing*, the perplexing *Barton Fink* and the madcap *The Big Lebowski* – and there's a handy multi-media reference at the back.

Noir Fiction by Paul Duncan

Noir has infiltrated our world, like some insidious disease, and we cannot get rid of it. The threads of its growth and development have been hinted at but no-one has yet tried to bind them together, to weave the whole picture. This book takes you down the dark highways of the Noir experience, and examines the history of Noir in literature, art, film, and pulps. Sensitive readers are warned – you may find the Noir world disturbing, terrifying and ultimately pessimistic. As well as an introductory essay, 19 of the most important authors are featured in more detail, including James M Cain, Cornell Woolrich, Horace McCoy, Jim Thompson, David Goodis, Charles Willeford, Derek Raymond and James Ellroy.

Woody Allen (Revised & Updated Edition) by Martin Fitzgerald

Woody Allen: Neurotic. Jewish. Funny. Inept. Loser. A man with problems. Or so you would think from the characters he plays in his movies. But hold on. Allen has written and directed 30 films. He may be a funny man, but he is also one of the most serious American filmmakers of his generation. This revised and updated edition includes *Sweet and Lowdown* and *Small Time Crooks*.

Orson Welles (Revised & Updated Edition) by Martin Fitzgerald

The popular myth is that after the artistic success of *Citizen Kane* it all went downhill for Orson Welles, that he was some kind of fallen genius. Yet, despite overwhelming odds, he went on to make great Films Noirs like *The Lady from Shanghai* and *Touch of Evil*. He translated Shakespeare's work into films with heart and soul (*Othello, Chimes at Midnight,*

Macbeth), and he gave voice to bitterness, regret and desperation in *The Magnificent Ambersons* and *The Trial*. Far from being down and out, Welles became one of the first cutting-edge independent filmmakers.

Film Noir by Paul Duncan
The laconic private eye, the corrupt cop, the heist that goes wrong, the femme fatale with the rich husband and the dim lover – these are the trademark characters of Film Noir. This book charts the progression of the Noir style as a vehicle for filmmakers who wanted to record the darkness at the heart of American society as it emerged from World War to the Cold War. As well as an introduction explaining the origins of Film Noir, seven films are examined in detail and an exhaustive list of over 500 Films Noir is included.

Alfred Hitchcock by Paul Duncan
More than 20 years after his death, Alfred Hitchcock is still a household name, most people in the Western world have seen at least one of his films, and he popularised the action movie format we see every week on the cinema screen. He was both a great artist and dynamite at the box office. This book examines the genius and enduring popularity of one of the most influential figures in the history of the cinema!

Index

The Pocket Essential Complete Stocklist

Slasher Movies
Spaghetti Westerns
Spike Lee
Stanley Kubrick
Steve McQueen
Steven Soderbergh
Steven Spielberg
Terry Gilliam
The Films of Graham Greene
The Marx Brothers
The Oscars
Tim Burton
Vampire Films
Vietnam War Movies
Woody Allen
Writing a Screenplay

History
Alchemy and Alchemists
American Civil War
American Indian Wars
Ancient Greece
Bohemian London
Jack the Ripper
Nazi War Trials
Nelson
Secret Societies
St. George
The Black Death
The Cathars
The Crusades
The Gnostics
The History Of Witchcraft

The Holy Grail
The Knights Templar

Ideas
Conspiracy Theories
Feminism
Freud And Psychoanalysis
Globalisation
Nietzsche
Nuclear Paranoia
Postmodernism
Psychogeography
Rise Of New Labour
The Universe
UFOs
Who Shot JFK?

Literature
Agatha Christie
Alan Moore
Creative Writing
Cyberpunk
F Scott Fitzgerald
Georges Simenon
Hitchhikers Guide
Literary Theory
Noir Fiction
Philip K Dick
Robert Crumb
Sherlock Holmes
Terry Pratchett
The Beat Generation
Tintin
William Shakespeare

Music

Bruce Springsteen
How To Succeed In The
Music Business
Jethro Tull
The Beastie Boys
The Beatles
The Madchester Scene

Sport

How to be a Sports Agent

Television

Doctor Who

Titles in **BOLD** are not yet published

For full details of prices and ISBNs see our website at
www.pocketessentials.com